D is for
DAD

Michael Heatley wrote the best-selling *The Dads' Book: For the Dad Who's Best at Everything*. He is the author of biographies of personalities ranging from Rolf Harris to Ricky Gervais, has interviewed celebrities from Dolly Parton to George Best and has written for numerous magazines including the *Radio Times* and the *Mail on Sunday* colour supplement. He is also the father of three children, now in their teens and twenties.

D is for
DAD

Michael Heatley

APPLE

First published in the UK in 2009 by
Apple Press
7 Greenland Street
London
NW1 0ND
www.apple-press.com

Conceived and produced by
Elwin Street Limited
144 Liverpool Road
London N1 1LA
www.elwinstreet.com

ISBN 978-1-84543-318-5

Designed by Jon Wainwright, Alchemedia Design
Illustrated by Micca/Dutch Uncle
Cover image: Mary Evans Picture Library

10 9 8 7 6 5 4 3 2 1

Printed in Singapore

Contents

Introduction

That becoming a father is a life-changing experience goes without saying. And you won't be alone in not feeling ready for it, or that maybe you'd like to have a few more weeks to think about it. Unfortunately, nature waits for no man (or woman). The biological fact is that you will become a dad when the new arrival wants you to. And when he does arrive, you have to take charge.

You've attended ante-natal classes and prepared for the birth, but it doesn't end there. If you have bad habits – excessive drinking or smoking – starting a family is the best motivation to cut down or stop. Healthy eating, cutting out the takeaways and fatty snacks and eating more fruit and vegetables is also something that will give you a much-needed boost in your new role as weary dad, as well as improving your lifestyle and setting a good example for your kids when they don't want to eat their broccoli.

Sleep will soon become a thing of the past. You'll inevitably suffer many a broken night before junior gets his head down and sleeps through the night on a regular basis. All that's certain is that, apart from a few smiles and shaken heads as you arrive at the office looking half-asleep, you'll have no respite from your career responsibilities. You'd better believe being a dad is a full-time job.

One of the most difficult things about becoming a father will be adding completely new responsibilities to your daily routine. Finding time for all your commitments may be a struggle – even if you're lucky enough to get paternity leave, the time will soon come when the demands at both ends of your life are going to stretch the poor man in the middle. That's what being a dad is all about.

From learning all the new practical tasks that accompany fatherhood to keeping the children entertained, from proving yourself as an adventurous outdoorsman to picking up the essential advanced-level skills, the advice in this book should help you face your new responsibilities without fear. In no time you'll be changing nappies with your eyes closed, amazing your young ones with your card tricks and balloon animals, teaching them to pitch a tent, and honing your advanced DIY skills.

The challenge ahead of you is one you've never faced before. You can read all you want, including this book, but you still won't be completely prepared for all that fatherhood brings. The good news is that it's always easier the second time around (not that you're even thinking about that yet), and that there are hidden reserves within us that ensure we rise to the task, even on the occasions we don't think we can. Once a dad, always a dad.

One thing's for sure – when the dust has settled and the incessant screaming has quietened to a contented gurgle, the respect you have for your own father is going to be at an all-time high. And remember, he's been through it all before, albeit a long time ago, so there's always someone you can turn to for friendly advice or just to vent your frustrations. Who knows, it could be the making of your relationship.

You don't get a medal, but you are now a fully-fledged member of the Dad's Brigade. Welcome to the club.

Practical Dad

- ❖ Holding a baby
- ❖ Changing a nappy
- ❖ Travelling with children
- ❖ Removing a splinter
- ❖ Cooking on Mum's night off

Young children are, in many ways, the biggest challenge for a dad. They can't tell you what to do, what's wrong or what happens next. So practicality is all-important. From learning how to hold a baby and change a nappy to administering basic first aid and installing a car seat, there are plenty of new things to learn. Keep it simple, follow these timely tips and you just may make it through the minefield that is first-time parenthood.

Holding a baby

This is important. For one, Mum isn't going to want to lug the baby around all the time. Second, it's actually quite nice to gather your tiny bundle of joy up in your arms and do a little bonding. In fact, research has shown that babies who are held most of the time get so much of their need for human contact and touch met early on that they cry less and become more independent, confident and happy, both as toddlers and in later years.

That said, holding an infant can be nerve-wracking. You might have shied away from holding babies before when friends or relatives thrust their 'adorable' infants into your arms. Lots of guys simply worry they're going to hurt a baby by holding too hard or dropping the poor little bundle. The crying doesn't help soothe nerves either.

Happily, there are several different techniques for holding a baby, including the traditional cradle hold, the stomach hold, the shoulder hold, the football hold and the forward-facing chair hold. You can also get yourself a sling or a baby carrier for those times you need both hands for a little home repair.

The one constant with any 'hold' is that you absolutely must support the baby's head and neck; until about six months an infant's neck muscles are not strong enough to hold his own head up.

Cradle hold

This is one of the easiest ways to hold a baby. Simply rest the baby's head in the inner bend of one arm with your forearm extending under his back and your hand on his lower back or bottom. Your other arm should run parallel to the first so that your hand can help support his head.

Stomach hold

For babies with excessive wind, being held stomach-down can be a relief. Simply slide one arm under the baby's tummy and rest his head in the palm of your hand. His legs and arms should hang down on either side of your arm. Bring your arm close to your stomach to help support him and use your other arm for extra stability.

Shoulder hold

A key hold for burping babies as well as a pretty comfortable one, the shoulder hold is one every dad should learn. Just wrap one arm under your baby's bottom while his stomach or chest rests against your chest and shoulder. Place your free hand on his back for support.

Football hold

Just as a rugby player tucks the ball under his arm as he runs down the field, you can tuck your baby under your arm (though you might not want to do any running). The baby will lie on his back along the length of one arm with his head in your hand and feet extending toward your back. This hold is best used by Mum while breastfeeding, but that doesn't mean you can't give it a try yourself.

Forward-facing chair hold

So-called because you use one hand to support the baby's bottom or legs while he leans back against your chest and shoulder as if sitting in a chair. Your free hand should be placed on the baby's stomach or chest to help support him and to keep him from flopping forward. This is a great hold when you're sitting down. It takes some practice to feel confident for long periods of standing up.

Slings and baby carriers

After about two months of carrying a baby around, you might start to feel a twinge in your lower back and shoulders – babies are small but they reach 7 kilograms (15 pounds) surprisingly quickly. You also might want to free up at least one arm to actually get something done while holding him. In that case, get yourself a baby sling that goes over one shoulder or buy a front baby carrier that straps over your shoulder and back. You might think you look silly with one of these things on – and you do. Just get used to it. You're a dad now.

Don't hold a baby too tight, but make sure you have a firm hold on him. You should be aware that babies — even the youngest ones — can push off and flop around quite a bit as they test out their forming muscles. You don't want him to be able to push off and out of your arms.

Preparing a bottle

If you find yourself – gasp! – alone with the baby while Mum is out with the girls making up for lost time, you'll need to know how to feed him. Obviously, you won't need a breast pump. Here's how to get a bottle ready for your young one. It's all the rage for modern mums and dads to use only bottled water for preparing infant formula. If you are concerned about the quality of your tap water, by all means use bottled water. Just remember that bottled water is not always sterilised, so this too needs to be boiled first.

You will need
❖ 4 x 125 ml baby bottles with nipples
❖ Boiled water
❖ Infant powdered formula mix

1 Before being left alone, make sure you have everything you need to feed your baby, in the form of baby bottles with nipples, a way to boil water and infant powdered formula mix.
2 Make sure the bottle and nipple are sterilised by running them through a hot dishwasher or by buying a bottle steriliser, which is basically a modified electric vegetable steamer. (Don't be inclined to modify your own.)
3 To make 500 ml of formula – enough for four feeds, depending on weight – boil at least 500 ml of water for about 5 minutes. You can keep formula in the refrigerator for about 48 hours after you've mixed it, and your young bottomless pit – er, baby – will surely have no problem going through this much.

4   Scoop out enough formula into each 125 ml bottle and add boiling water to all. The instructions on every pack of infant formula will tell you the appropriate ratio of mix to water and it's very important to get it right. Too little water could upset your baby's stomach and too much will dilute the mixture so that he doesn't get the right amount of nutrition. Mix each bottle with a sterilised spoon.

5   If you need to feed him right away, cool the mixture down first by submerging the bottle in iced water to just under the screw-top nipple. Turn the bottle in the iced water to increase the cooling process. Test the temperature of the formula by putting a few drops of it on the inside of your wrist. It should be body temperature (just like Mum's breast milk), no cooler and certainly no hotter.

6   Heating up a bottle out of the fridge should be done by heating up water on the stove and putting the bottle in the hot water. Never use a microwave, which can heat the formula unevenly and potentially burn your young one's mouth.

Safety in the home

When you have a newborn – say up to six months old – you don't have to worry about him sticking a stray chopstick in the wall plug. Firstly, he can't crawl or walk, and secondly, where on earth is he going to find a chopstick? What you do have to worry about is making sure that he will be secure in the places he spends most of his time. It's when he starts crawling and walking that you'll want to bring out the plug protectors and hide the poison.

Safety in the home: zero to six months

- ❖ First, make sure you've constructed the cot and changing table correctly and securely. Don't risk the furniture collapsing while the baby is in or on it.
- ❖ If you have a changing table, make sure it has some kind of edge protection or strap-down belt so that he can't roll off onto the floor. Don't ever leave the baby unattended though, even if you do have protection in place.
- ❖ Just in case you take the above precautions and he still rolls off, put a thick rug down to cushion the impact.
- ❖ In an infant's cot, it's important not to fill it with anything soft and cuddly. Babies can suffocate on fluffy blankets, pillows, over-soft mattresses, stuffed animals and the like.
- ❖ Make sure the slats on the cot are close enough together so that he doesn't get his head stuck between them. This could be an issue for old cots.

Safety in the home: six months to a year

❖ Place plastic plug outlet protectors in each and every plug socket around the house. You may find it annoying to have to pull these things out when you want to plug in the vacuum cleaner, but it's worth it. Besides, almost nothing will be as easy as it used to be now that you're a parent.

❖ Put locks on all cupboards so that small hands can't get to what's inside, like the cleaning products. Even then it's a good idea to put any toxic cleaners or spare poison into locked upper cupboards, just in case.

❖ Consider padding all sharp corners (coffee tables, brick fireplaces, etc.). You won't win any interior design awards but your infant will avoid regular dangerous bumps and collisions.

❖ Place safety gates or barriers at the top and bottom of stairs.

❖ Never leave small objects or plastic bags, which can cause choking, within a baby's reach.

❖ Don't put your baby down alone on a waterbed, beanbag or soft blanket that could cover his face and cause suffocation.

❖ Make sure you use the harness properly every time you put your baby in a highchair.

❖ Set the temperature of your hot water system to 49°C (120°F) to prevent accidental scalding.

❖ Put non-skid backing under any slippery rugs.

❖ Remove tall precarious stacks of CDs, not only because they'll fall over on tiny heads but also because it's no fun having to reorganise your music collection.

Stop the crying

It is normal for small babies to cry, and does not mean that you are failing as a dad – it is a baby's way of communicating that he wants something, and it's normally something fairly simple. He doesn't have many requirements at this point, and his needs will generally be confined to nappy changes, feeding, sleeping and any discomfort he is feeling such as teething. So if your baby is crying there are a few simple things you can check first to ensure that his basic needs are being met.

Top ways to get your baby to stop crying

- ❖ Check the nappy. No one likes to wear soggy underwear.
- ❖ Try feeding the little rascal.
- ❖ He may need to be burped – try placing your baby over your shoulder and gently rubbing or patting his back.
- ❖ It might be that your youngster is tired, especially if he missed a regular nap, and needs help getting to sleep.
- ❖ A rocking motion is soothing, so try rocking him gently in a chair or cot, take a stroll with him in the baby carrier, or take him for a drive.
- ❖ Check that he is comfortable and not too hot or cold.
- ❖ If he is teething, give him a teething ring.
- ❖ Swaddle him snugly in a blanket and hold him close to offer warmth and comfort.
- ❖ Try singing or reading to him – the sound of your familiar voice will be soothing.

Change a nappy

In the first weeks of your baby's life, you will change hundreds of nappies. Soon you'll be able to swap a dry one for a wet one with your eyes closed. You need to change him as soon as possible, as leaving him in a soggy nappy can cause irritation and nappy rash. But before you master the art of the nappy change, you're first going to have to learn to steady a squirming baby and avoid getting peed on while making sure the nappy fits comfortably but snugly.

You will also need to decide if you are opting for cloth or disposable nappies – often a great debate in parenting circles. Cloth nappies are the cheaper option, and may cause less nappy rash, while also being the greener option – millions of disposable nappies are thrown away every day, while cloth nappies are recyclable. On the other hand cloth nappies require a lot of laundering and disposables are often much more convenient – if you are away from home, for example, you will probably want to just change the dirty nappy and get rid of it. It will be up to you to decide which option suits you (and your baby) best.

1 Before you get started, prepare everything you will need and place it nearby – nappies, wipes, rash ointments and nappy pail. You shouldn't ever leave a baby unattended, especially high up on a surface where he could fall off, so you should keep one hand on him at all times.
2 Lay him gently on his back on a changing table, floor, or any other firm surface. Make sure the surface is covered with some kind of washable blanket or waterproof material.

If you're planning to use cloth nappies, look at the options available instead of safety pins – they always end up pricking both dad and baby. Instead you can use nappy covers that hold cloth nappy in place like a pair of plastic underwear and fasten across the front with hook and loop. They come in small, medium and large sizes, and can be ordered on the Internet.

3   Take off the nappy by loosening the fasteners on each side, holding his feet in one hand and lifting his rear end off the surface, while at the same time, pulling the nappy away from his bottom.

4   If you're dealing with more than just a wet nappy, fold the front of the nappy under his bottom so that the contents are covered. Don't let go of his feet or you'll have more than a bottom to clean. (If you have a baby boy, take care to cover his penis with a cloth, or you may get peed on.)

5   Gently clean your baby by wiping from front to back with a baby wipe or a soft, warm, wet cloth. This is particularly important for baby girls so that you avoid the possibility of spreading infections. Do a thorough job and be sure to remove all faeces.

6   You may want to use a cream or ointment to soothe or prevent nappy rash – ask a pediatrician for advice on recommended treatments.

7   When you've cleaned up and applied any ointment, hold his feet in one hand, lift his bottom off the surface, and slide a fresh nappy under it.

8   Fold the front of the nappy between his legs over his front and fasten one side of the nappy and then the other. Make sure the nappy fits snugly around his hips and that the tape or Velcro isn't too tight and cutting into his skin.

9   Dispose of the used nappy and wash your hands thoroughly.

Travelling with a baby

Travelling with babies younger than one year old can be both enlightening and harrowing, and a lot of it has to do with the method of travel. Some babies love car travel and some don't. When they don't, driving is really stressful. Imagine being stuck in traffic while your baby is screaming in the back seat. Not fun. Not fun at all.

Whatever way you choose to transport your baby, just make sure you take along the essentials like nappies, baby wipes and a blanket. Longer trips require an astonishing amount of stuff, even if it's just an overnighter. You have to bring blankets, cloths, favourite stuffed animals, toys, a portable cot, bottles, sterilisers, powders, ointments and a thousand changes of clothes. Makes you realise why families buy cars with large boots.

The dos and don'ts of driving with a baby

- ❖ Do learn to love nursery rhymes played over and over and over.
- ❖ Do learn to drive safely even when your baby's screams are piercing your innermost being.
- ❖ Do be prepared to have to stop every two hours or so.
- ❖ Don't drive faster so that you can make it to your destination before your baby wakes up.
- ❖ Don't drive with one hand while using the other to play with him in the back seat.
- ❖ Don't curse, yell or otherwise succumb to road rage.
- ❖ Don't fall asleep because you were up with the baby all night.
- ❖ Don't fall asleep because you were out with the guys all night.
- ❖ Don't get a flat tyre.

Travel by plane

Flying with a baby and without Mum is not recommended – but if you have to do it, you have to do it. Just make sure you are prepared. Have a checklist ready of all the baby kit you need, and prepare to become the most unpopular person on the flight. Travelling by plane with your own child is a new experience. We've all been on a crowded plane with a baby who won't stop crying, and we've all imagined stuffing that baby and his good-for-nothing father in the plane's bathroom and locking the door. And that's the nice version. Well, that was before we had kids. Now that you're a dad and you're flying, the tables have turned. It's you who will be held responsible for any crying, and it's your baby that every passenger who gets on the plane will stare at with dread. Luckily not all babies cry and squeal on planes. Many just sleep through the whole experience as if they were at home.

Unfortunately, lots of people who fly have never had kids themselves. That's why the air passengers who glare and shake their heads at you when your baby is upset don't know (and don't care) that babies cry for a reason. The chances are if your baby is crying he's hungry, he has a wet nappy, or he's in some discomfort, which on planes is likely to come from the altitude change and the pressure it exerts on tiny ears. That's why it's essential to get him to suck on something – preferably Mum's breast – while taking off and landing. This will allow their ears to 'pop' (i.e. it equalises the pressure inside the ear with that of the air outside the eardrum), thereby relieving the most common and most painful reason for his tears. Now you just have to contend with the cramped quarters, the inability to lie down and the stress of boarding and getting off.

To make sure your flight is as stress-free as possible, the following are some tips and precautions you can take before you fly and once you are in the air.

How to fly successfully with a baby

- ❖ Avoid busy times of year.
- ❖ Stroll your baby to the gate, at which point the crew will check your pushchair for the flight, handing it back to you when you land.
- ❖ Try to get a seat as close to the front as possible.
- ❖ Befriend a doting stranger who looks like they would love to hold a baby for the Bangkok to New York stretch.
- ❖ Reconsider flying with sick babies or babies with hayfever – congestion can block ear canals and make it impossible for your baby's ears to equalise.
- ❖ Don't bring a lot of carry-on luggage that you have to juggle along with a baby.
- ❖ Bring extra dummies, bottles, or whatever else you think he will suck on successfully.
- ❖ Accept any help crew members wish to bestow.

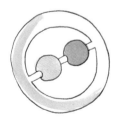

What to pack

Taking your offspring away from the four walls of home is something no dad should do on a whim. Planning on the scale of a military operation is crucial. Keep a checklist of all the essential pieces of kit for travelling with small children, from the basic essentials such as a first aid kit to entertainments such as a favourite toy. Make sure that you will be equipped to deal with any eventuality or demand so that the trip doesn't end in tears.

Travel checklist

- ❖ **Wipes and tissues.** Keep it clean!
- ❖ **Blankets.** To sit on/lie on/be warmed up by – a blanket is an invaluable piece of equipment when travelling.
- ❖ **Change of clothes.** For any number of reasons, this is a must, and not just for extended travels.
- ❖ **Drinks.** The first cry of the dissatisfied offspring is often 'I'm thirsty!' (Well, right after 'Are we there yet?', anyway).
- ❖ **Healthy snacks.** Giving children food will distract them from long drives, sibling fights and boredom.
- ❖ **Plastic bags.** To clean up any mess or rubbish – but keep away from little hands for safety reasons.
- ❖ **Games/books/comics.** Always take some form of entertainment – for the journey and for when you get to your destination and it rains!
- ❖ **First aid kit.** Prepare for the worst and you won't be disappointed.

Safety in the car

Unlike 35 years ago, when children were allowed to roam freely inside cars with or without seatbelts on, nowadays there are car seats and a host of rules that go with them. And this is a good thing. Car seats are sturdy and designed to save lives if you were to get into an accident. Remember that the seatbelts that come with your car are designed for adults and are not good enough to keep your child safe. It won't be until your baby has grown to a strapping 1.45 metres (4 foot 9 inches) and 36 kilograms (80 pounds) that you can use just a normal seatbelt.

Don't drive around without your baby strapped into his seat, even if you're just popping down to the corner shop. It's just not smart. You could get him seriously injured and get yourself arrested for negligence. Also, remember that when you're driving with a baby, you're going to stop a lot to feed and change nappies, and that's going to add time to your trip. Again, planning will help make your trip far more stress- and frustration-free. You might also get to places on time.

Installing a car seat

There are varying rules and regulations when it comes to securing a car seat before buckling your child in, but some general rules do apply everywhere. Also, each car seat is going to come with a set of detailed instructions. Read and follow them to the letter.

Car seat pointers

❖ Infants and toddlers under 9 kilos (20 pounds) should face towards the back of the car, as it is safer than facing the front.

❖ Many car seats have built-in levels so you can ensure the seat isn't leaning too far forward or back, which is also important if you're in an accident. However, if your baby's head keeps flopping forward when he goes to sleep in the car, it's okay to tilt the seat back slightly more. You can do this by putting a folded-up towel under the front part of the seat.

❖ Try to get a safe car seat that has a base and a removable seat that you can pop in and out when he is asleep. It's amazingly helpful, as strapping car seats in with seatbelts is a real nuisance.

❖ All kids under about 18 kilograms (40 pounds) should have a three-point harness seatbelt. After that they can go to car booster seats and use the car's over-the-shoulder seatbelt.

❖ The middle of the back seat is always the safest place to put a car seat. Make sure the base of the seat is flat. Thread the seatbelt through and buckle it. (Read the instructions that come with the car seat to find out exactly where to put the belt).

❖ Pull the shoulder belt tight to check that it locks. If the seatbelts in your car aren't the locking kind, invest in a locking clip that fits onto the car seatbelt just over the buckle.

❖ Many car seats now come with tether systems, which consist of a belt that secures the seat to a permanent metal anchor welded to the frame of the car. Usually tether anchors can be found on the floor board in front of the back seat or on the rear dash behind the seat, and are used instead of car seatbelts.

First aid

Babies are prone to all kinds of cuts, bumps, scrapes, bug bites and other minor injuries. But this is nothing compared with when they start crawling and especially after they start wobbling around on two feet. You might like to show off your childhood scars in the bar with your pals, but your baby won't be so delighted to show you his bumps and bruises and he'll darn well let you know when he's hurt himself on the edge of the coffee table.

Minor injuries are a part of life as your baby begins to explore his world (albeit in an often haphazard way). But he needs you to look out for him with more than just a soothing word and a cuddle. Now is not the time to tell him to buck up and to take it on the chin 'cause the world ain't a friendly place. Now is the time to accept that he is prone to scrapes, to protect him as much as you can without stifling his space to explore, and to brush up on your strapping Dad-to-the-rescue routine. Think of it as a chance for your little one to begin looking up to you in awe and wonder as their hero. You know it won't last long.

Here are some words of advice for how to treat more common, minor ailments.

How to remove a splinter

A splinter is a painful but unavoidable by-product of the outdoor life, DIY, any number of things, but you will be much more used to them than your child is. Be firm but gentle, and do it as quickly as possible.

1   You can try digging it out with a needle and yanking it out with tweezers, but your child probably won't let you near a splinter again and there are easier and less painful ways.

2   If it has not gone too far in, firmly press a piece of packing tape over the splinter and then remove the tape sharply. Or, take some wood glue and put a drop on the splinter. Smear it and let it dry. After it is dry, peel off in the direction the splinter went in (so you don't break it off) and the glue will pull the splinter out for you.

3   Alternatively, wash the area, then apply a paste of water and a quarter-teaspoon of baking soda, and cover it for 24 hours. When the bandage is removed the splinter will be sticking out of the skin and can be taken out easily.

How to treat cuts and scrapes

There's not much you can do to prevent your child from getting cuts and scrapes. You'll just have to accept that your child will fall down and bump into things on a regular basis. All you can do is be there to pick up the pieces and kiss it better.

1   If the cut is bleeding, apply direct pressure until the bleeding stops.

2   Wash the area with warm water and soap to remove any dirt. If dirt is present in the cut, try to get it out by running warm water over the cut to flush it out. If there is dirt deep within the cut, don't try to dig it out as you may cause more damage.

3   Cover the area with a plaster.

4   If the cut or graze is minor, uncover the area at night to let the wound dry out and heal faster. Cover again in the morning if need be. If you notice any signs of infection, such as redness, swelling or pus, take your baby to the doctor.

Burns

From hot coffee or tea to a long day at the beach, babies have the chance of burning themselves more often than we'd like to think. There are some who say that once they burn themselves they won't do it again, but that sounds shaky to me (and perhaps even criminal). Does that mean we shouldn't put a screen in front of the fireplace or we should leave the oven door open with a baby in the room? Not a chance. A better option is to get your baby to pre-school age and beyond without ever burning himself. At that point you can reason with them and tell them it will hurt. Simply put, avoid burns at all costs.

When you are cooking (yes, we dads do literally put food on the table at times), drinking hot coffee, barbecuing, ironing (okay, this might be a stretch), or doing anything else that involves flame or heat, keep a watchful eye on him. If he gets too close to something, a quick, loud 'hey' or 'no' will definitely get his attention. He might start crying because you startled him, but it's better than a burn that smarts for the rest of the evening.

In fact, the sooner your baby learns to heed your words and pick up on the attitude with which you say them, the better. You only have one pair of hands, and sometimes you won't be able to catch your baby as quickly as he might pull at a cord or touch a heater. We men aren't always the best at multi-tasking, but becoming a dad is a quick way to develop the skill of having eyes in the back of your head. The goal here is to foster a relationship with your baby in which he knows that Dad is looking out for him. He should know that obeying Dad's instructions and heeding his verbal warnings are really good ideas.

How to treat burns

1 Fill up a sink with cool tap water and soak burned fingers, hands or feet until he calms down and the pain seems to go away.
2 If soaking is impractical, use cold compresses (a cool wash cloth soaked with tap water will work fine) until the pain subsides.
3 For sunburns, use cold compresses for about 10 minutes at a time, roughly three times a day or any time your baby seems troubled by the burn.
4 After applying the compresses, apply moisturising cream or calamine lotion.
5 In both cases, consider giving him paracetamol or some other pain reliever to make him more comfortable. It's always good to consult your doctor before doing this.

Dos and don'ts

❖ Do prevent sunburns by keeping babies fully covered in lightweight clothing and sun hats.
❖ Don't put ice directly on any kind of burn as it can damage the skin (frostbite) and make things worse.
❖ Don't use petroleum jelly on a sunburn because it clogs pores, seals out air and does not help the healing process.

A rough guide to discipline

As a dad, you want family life to go smoothly and with a smile at all times. You want to be a happy family. But think back to your own youth and you'll soon remember that discipline, however firmly applied, made you the man you are today.

Children, even young adults, always need to know where their boundaries are, but it's natural they will push at them. Your aim is to be firm, fair and above all consistent. And be sure to praise and reward good behaviour as well as condemn the opposite.

- ❖ **0–2 year olds.** A firm 'no' if he heads towards something dangerous or inappropriate. Aggression or food throwing can be punished with a short 'time out' in an appointed place. Always explain in a kindly way what you're doing and why – it all goes in.
- ❖ **3–5 year olds.** Your child is now beginning to understand the link between his actions and the consequences – good and bad – so this is a very important time. A chart on the fridge door could be used to register good and bad behaviour, and rewards given.
- ❖ **6–8 year olds.** The most difficult age in some ways. Ensure you follow through on your decisions but don't go over the top in punishment – he needs to see the end of the tunnel or there's no incentive to improve. You are still learning how to administer discipline, so don't make threats in haste. Let yourself cool down for two minutes, then take action.
- ❖ **9–12 year olds.** You can now start handing out rewards and responsibilities in exchange for good behaviour, such as allowing walks to shops and schools (if safe and appropriate). As school

sets demands in terms of homework assignments, make sure
these are met – or that, if they are not, the lesson is learned and
consequence accepted.

❖ **13–15 year olds.** Hopefully, by now your relationship with your
child is strong enough to withstand the teenage years where
mistakes are still made but hopefully lessons learned. It's still
important to have clearly defined boundaries, though – the
biggest battle can be reasoning with your teen and talking through
the consequences of their carelessness. Dad may be the authority
figure, but he can still be upset, so don't be afraid to show your
own vulnerability.

❖ **16 years and onwards.** Your child is now a young adult and you'd
better believe he knows it! But he's still your responsibility, and
you'll find that the carrot often works better than the stick.
Continue offering rewards such as a slightly later curfew for
prompt returns home rather than an earlier one for bad
behaviour. Once he turns 18, you will be equals, so this is a good
time to start digesting that fact, difficult though it may sometimes
be. And when he himself becomes a parent – not too soon,
hopefully! – he'll thank you for your example.

Pocket money

The Bank of Dad is always open. You can get some bang for your buck by putting your children to work. They learn the value of money, you get a bit of free time (well, perhaps not free exactly, but your wallet should be able to withstand the damage). Children respond well to financial rewards, so it's a good way to get them to help out around the house and teach them about the concept of earning money. If they're too young to spend what they earn, open a building society account for them and get them saving for that rainy day.

- ❖ **5–7 year olds.** A good starting point is little jobs like tidying up the toys in their room and putting their dirty clothes in the laundry basket. Once a little bit older, they can help their younger brothers and sisters get dressed and clean their teeth. They'll be so proud to be wage earners any piece of silver will be gratefully accepted. Ah, the innocence of youth!

- ❖ **8–11 year olds.** Once they can be trusted not to break things, they can progress to washing the dishes and making their own sandwiches. If you are lucky you can get away with paying your eight year-old a comparatively modest sum to do several sinks full of dishes. Beware, though, the novelty will wash off sooner or later.

- ❖ **12 years and upwards.** If the thought of cutting the grass or washing the car spoils your weekend, let the children take the strain! As taking your car to the carwash costs money, they can expect a similar fee for performing the task on your driveway.

Teach children about the value of money early on so that they know where it comes from and that it doesn't just magically appear from Dad's wallet. Introduce the idea of saving money by buying your children a piggy bank and encouraging them to save up their pennies rather than spending them all at once.

First day at school

It's a landmark day for children and parents alike. But a bit of forethought can take much of the fear factor away. Above all, don't dismiss your child's fears – things that seem obvious to an adult can appear as obstacles to a five year old.

In the weeks before school starts

* Explain where he'll be going, how long for and what he'll be doing (emphasise the things he enjoys doing).
* Make sure he plays with children of a similar age to develop social skills.
* Read books about starting school or use favourite toys to role-play going to school to get him interested and excited.
* Play games that involve taking turns, sitting down for short periods of time or speaking in front of a group.
* Involve your child in choosing things like schoolbags or uniforms.
* Visit the school with your child so he becomes familiar with the buildings and local area.
* Make sure he can feed himself, use the toilet, go up and down stairs and dress himself. If he is struggling, don't do everything for him – help him learn for himself.
* Leave your child with a relation or friend for a few hours. It will give your child confidence knowing you'll be back!
* If your child will be starting school with a friend from any pre-school groups you've attended, see if you can all go together on the big day.

School reports

Rudyard Kipling advised us to treat triumph and disaster just the same. In that spirit, the school report should be regarded as a 'snapshot' of your child. What's more, it's a snapshot taken by someone else – their teacher or teachers. That means it's an objective view, but not the only one. The teacher knows how they are at school, you know how they are at home. The 'real' kid is somewhere in between. Here are some tips to avoid tension.

Discussing a report

If your child has a good report, acknowledge it. Let him know you're proud of his achievements. But effort is just as important, so have realistic expectations about what a good report should be.

If his report suggests that he could be doing better, don't approach it in a negative way. Try to be encouraging and reassure him that poor grades don't mean he is a failure. Suggest ways that he could improve, but don't compare him to more successful friends or siblings.

Encourage good habits

It's never too early to learn good study habits. Make learning a part of their domestic timetable and take an interest in their homework throughout the year. A small gift like a CD or a meal out can reward a good report. But don't use this as a bribe, and be aware of other siblings who may not have done as well. Remind your children that success in school lays the groundwork for future success. The sacrifices they make will pay off later in life.

Sandwiches for kids

Having some tried and tested sandwich ideas are a good idea if you're suddenly expected to rustle up lunch or snacks for the kids.

Chicken salad sandwich

You will need

- 200 g (½ lb) chopped, cooked chicken meat
- Onion or celery, finely chopped (optional)
- 1 teaspoon lemon juice
- 2 tablespoons mayonnaise
- Salt and pepper to taste
- Lettuce
- Bread

Just mix all of the ingredients together and serve between two slices of bread, or toast if preferred.

Tuna salad sandwich

You will need

- 170 g (6 oz) can of tuna fish
- ⅓ cup of cottage cheese
- 2 tablespoons mayonnaise
- 1 teaspoon Dijon mustard
- Salad ingredients of your choice (try lettuce and sliced tomatoes)
- Bread

Canned tuna packed in water rather than oil is the healthier option. Drain the tuna, combine all the ingredients together and serve between two slices of bread.

Egg salad sandwich

You will need

- ❖ I large hard-boiled egg, peeled and chopped
- ❖ I–2 tablespoons mayonnaise
- ❖ Chopped salad onion
- ❖ Chopped celery

- ❖ Pinch of curry powder to taste
- ❖ Salt and pepper
- ❖ Lettuce
- ❖ Bread

1 Boil at least an inch of water in a saucepan, and add a small amount of vinegar to the water in case the shells crack.

2 Put the eggs in, bring to the boil, remove from heat and cover.
3 After 12 minutes drain water, cool and shell eggs.
4 Mash egg with mayonnaise, onion and celery. Season.
5 Toast bread (if required), spread egg mixture and add lettuce.
6 Slice in half and serve.

Dad's signature dish

Once upon a time it was safer if Dad was not allowed into the kitchen. Now, with celebrity chefs more common than McDonald's, you can't avoid males lurking round the hob dying to try their hand. Even if that's not you, then you should still try to have at least one signature dish. It can be something simple and homely or complicated and show-offy; just remember, you're striking a blow for equality.

❖ **Steak**. Anything grilled is right up a dad's street. Barbecue ribs with a special sauce is another meaty treat; keep your sauce recipe a closely guarded secret

❖ **Meatloaf or meatballs**. Down-home and filling is the watchword here. The occasional unexpected added ingredient such as Worcester sauce or Parmesan cheese can add an unexpected kick and enhance respect.

❖ **Lasagne**. A safe standby for dads who fancy themselves as Italian masters of their house.

❖ **Stuffed peppers.** This might be a bit fancy for some, but it can also be used as a starter if Mum wants to cook too.

❖ **Macaroni cheese**. A nice and simple but satisfying recipe for the culinarily challenged dad. Cauliflower cheese is a variation with a healthy twist, but don't cook the cauli too long!

❖ **Anything with chicken**. Poultry's a good standby. After all, who can mess up chicken? (Just make sure it's cooked all the way through!) Southern fried coating can even be applied from a packet by any dad who gets scared by kitchen appliances. Just put it in a plastic bag, shake and bake.

Recipes for Mum's night off

If the cook of the household is out with friends, at an evening class or you're giving her a well earned break, you may have to take on the culinary chores for a night, and the kids may eventually get bored of your one perfected signature dish. In which case you will need some back up recipes. It can appear daunting at first, but we dads are made of tough stuff – and the sense of achievement will make the kitchen challenge worthwhile.

Here are three quick and easy dad-friendly standbys.

Nachos

At their simplest, nachos are simply a layer of tortilla chips with melted cheddar cheese and tomato sauce on the top. Added extras like refried beans, salsa, guacamole and sour cream are optional and will only be insisted on by your older offspring. (The cook, of course, is entitled to whatever extras he pleases.)

You will need
- ❖ Large packet tortilla chips
  – the thickest you can find
- ❖ 250 g (½ lb) cheddar
  cheese, grated
- ❖ Salsa
- ❖ Guacamole
- ❖ Sour cream

1 Arrange an overlapping layer of tortilla chips on a large plate. This should be a couple of chips thick.
2 Sprinkle the grated cheese evenly over the top of the chips. Then add salsa to taste.

3   Heat in the microwave oven for 60 seconds or until the cheese
    is melted.
4   Serve with generous dollops of salsa, sour cream and/or
    guacamole if desired.

Tacos

You can put almost anything in a taco. That makes it a great use of
leftovers, a fact that will bring a smile to the face of any cost-
conscious dad. Shells can be purchased from all supermarkets,
assuming that making tortillas is beyond the ability of most of us.

You will need
- 500 g (1 lb) meat (chicken,   - Packet taco shells
  beef, or pork)   - Salsa (homemade
- Lettuce   or prepared)
- Cheddar cheese, grated

1   Heat up the frying pan on medium-high heat and prepare your
    meat ingredient. Slice the lettuce and grate the cheese.
2   When the pan is hot, fry the meat – this can be cooked from
    scratch (minced beef) or warmed through (already cooked
    leftovers).
3   Open up each taco and add the hot ingredients, making sure the
    temperature is not too warm for your 'customers'. Let the children
    add the cheese, lettuce, and salsa. Salsa can be made from onions
    and tomatoes, finely chopped.

Spaghetti Bolognese

This good old standby can be served with salad (the healthy option kids don't usually like) or garlic bread (which they inevitably do).

You will need

- Minced beef
- One tin chopped tomatoes, or tube tomato paste
- Fried onions
- Garlic bread
- Spaghetti (one handful per person)
- Grated cheese (parmesan for preference)

1 Put meat in frying pan and cook gently and continuously until no pink is seen.
2 Make your sauce by combining tomatoes and onions, seasoning to taste, and heat until it thickens. (Lazy dads can cheat by buying pre-prepared pasta sauce.)
3 Mix sauce in with the meat after draining off excess fat.
4 Place garlic bread in oven for allotted time.
5 Add desired amount of dry spaghetti to a large pan of boiling water.
6 Cook spaghetti for the time recommended on the packet.
7 Drain spaghetti in a sieve or colander.
8 Place spaghetti on plates, topping with meat and sauce mixture.
9 Apply cheese to taste.
10 Get garlic bread out of oven and serve on the side.

Entertaining Dad

- ❖ Trick-or-treating
- ❖ Making balloon animals
- ❖ Learning to juggle
- ❖ Creating a flip book
- ❖ Becoming a ventriloquist

Even in these days of technology where children have so many things to entertain them, with DVDs, satellite television and computer games, there are times when only a dad and his unique methods of entertaining will do. There are plenty of tried, tested and (thank goodness!) cheap ways to keep your brood contented, whether playing peek-a-boo, fooling them with card tricks, or telling them a story. Sometimes the old pastimes are the best – and, who knows, they may pass them on to their own children in years to come. Until then, try playing these games with your children and enjoy the bonding time you spend together.

Peek-a-boo

Through the clever use of his hands, Dad appears and disappears. Here's one for the very young – simple yet highly popular. First, fix your baby with a steady gaze to gain their attention. Now bring up your hands to cover your face, then open them like a set of double doors, revealing a beaming dad. Close them and after the briefest of pauses, open again. Your baby's merriment will know no bounds. In fact you may be surprised by how long a very junior member of your family will find this amusing. Indeed, after but a few short minutes, you may find your enthusiasm lagging considerably faster than theirs. In this case, it may be useful to rely on the 'hand-off' manoeuver. Picking up the child, you turn and hand her off to her mother.

Spoon on nose

We know that we shouldn't encourage our kids to play with their food. But to play with implements, ahh, that is a different story. While you'll hear fans of this jolly jest argue the merits of sterling over silver plate, pretty much any teaspoon will do. Here's how it works. First, lick the tip of your finger and rub the end of your nose. Next, breathe on the spoon once or twice so that it fogs up. Take the teaspoon, tilt your head back slightly and balance the spoon on your nose. Pure mirth. Never in the history of father-inspired mirth has so much been generated by so little.

Detachable finger

Simple perhaps, but a timeless classic, and one of the fundamental building blocks in any dad-as-entertainer's repertoire. Of course it's not foolproof, so do practice it in front of a mirror until you have it right before trying it out on your children. Bend your thumb inward and fold the index finger over it to cover its knuckle completely. On your other hand, curl your index finger back so it looks like a stub. Tuck the stub of this finger under the index finger that's holding back the thumb on the first hand. It should look like the finger is passing behind the index finger and emerging on the other side.

Now, assuming a suitable pretext, call your children's attention to yourself – 'Hey, look' works well. Then pull back the left hand, giving the impression that you have pulled off the top of your index finger. Bask in the general hilarity.

The fountain of Mentos

This trick has an unforgettably messy outcome. It uses two popular modern treats: Mentos, those chewy mints from the Netherlands, and diet cola. Spectacular and educational, it provides us with a vivid demonstration of the way in which carbon dioxide, found in all carbonated drinks, can, with the aid of the dissolving sugar coating and gum arabic contained in Mentos, sunder the tight bonds that typically hold water molecules together. Which conclusively proves – uh, something. Here is another activity that might well wait until Mum has left the building.

1 Take a bottle of diet cola (diet versions work well and are not terribly sticky, an advantage that will become clear in a moment), open it, and set it down in an open space, ideally outdoors. Make sure that the ground is solid and level so the bottle will not fall over.

2 Next, unwrap all the Mentos. You want to drop them in the carbonated drink. But not one at a time – they need to hit the fluid virtually all at once, which is harder than you might think. One good way to do this is to rig sort of a paper tube to hold them all. Keep the end shut by pinching it with your thumb and forefinger and then hold it over the mouth of the bottle.

3 Release them, stand back, and behold your very own cola-flavored equivalent of the water features of Versailles, Rome's magnificent Trevi fountain, or Las Vegas's fabulous Bellagio Hotel, as a plume of fizzy diet drink rockets skyward.

What's this nose, then?

Dad magically steals – and then restores – his child's olfactory organ. A favorite of the older set, this is nonetheless well worth learning as a starter jest for any dad who wishes to entertain his children. It is really a variation on the finger-removal trick. Announce to your audience that you can pull their nose off. Reach up and hold the nose between index and middle knuckles of one hand, and give it a slight pinch. As you withdraw your hand, tuck the tip of your thumb in between the curled-over first and second fingers, so that the protruding end resembles the tip of the nose, miraculously and hilariously removed. A jest almost Zen-like in its purity.

Playing Father Christmas

Some people measure childhood from birth to when they first hear a rumour that Santa does not actually exist – so tread lightly on your children's dreams.

- ❖ Get the traditional fur-trimmed red costume, matching hat and black buckled boots. Don't forget the white beard.
- ❖ Take a bite out of the cookie they left for you – and it would be rude not to drink that glass of sherry or whiskey.
- ❖ Remember to put an orange or satsuma in each and every stocking you pin to the fireplace.
- ❖ If those little eyes should happen to flutter open, beat a dignified retreat with the occasional muttered 'ho ho ho'.

Trick-or-treating

Trick-or-treating happens on or around Halloween (31st October) with children going from house to house in costumes (which a prepared parent will have made well in advance) asking for treats such as confectionery with the question 'Trick or treat?' The tradition dates back to the Christmas wassailing of the Middle Ages, but the modern world isn't quite as innocent. Here are some tips to make sure it goes off without tears.

- ❖ Feed them a meal beforehand so that they won't want to eat so many sweets 'on the run'.
- ❖ Plan in advance – map out a route in daylight that keeps well away from roadworks, busy streets or similar obstacles.
- ❖ Stay with them and keep track of everyone in the group. Unless your children are teenagers, lurk (un)menacingly at the gate.
- ❖ Road safety. Don't let them stray too far ahead and impress the need for sensible behaviour near cars.
- ❖ Only visit houses that have lights on – old people and others' privacy should be respected.
- ❖ Inspect the sweets before eating – any with opened wrappers should be thrown away for safety's sake.
- ❖ Bring a bottle of water. All this trick-or-treating can get little wizards and witches hot and bothered.
- ❖ Have a pre-arranged time limit – by nine o'clock, at the latest, they will be more than ready to return home with their haul.

Making a bow and arrow

Making and shooting bows and arrows is a great sharing activity for dads and their children. Of course these arrows don't have actual arrowheads, but you should still lecture your kids about safety rules before giving this a go.

You will need
- A penknife
- Straight lengths of wood 60 cm (2 ft) long, for arrow shafts
- Feathers
- A straight length of strong, springy wood 1.2 m (4 ft) long, and about 2 cm (3⁄4 in) thick, for the bow
- 90 cm (3 ft) of cord or some type of tough string

To make the arrows

1 Make the arrow shafts as straight as possible by cutting off twigs and stripping away the bark. Sharpen one end to a point with a knife.
2 Cut a notch in the other end, about 0.5 cm (1⁄4 in) deep, so that you can fit the arrow on the bowstring.
3 Cut a feather in half, and cut each half into 1 cm (1⁄2 in) lengths. Tie three of these to the notched end of your arrow.

To make the bow

1 Check that the wood is free of knots or limbs. Scrape it down so that the wood is smooth, and trim it to be a little thinner at the ends. Take note of the natural curve of the wood – scrape from the side that will face you when you use the bow, or it will break the

first time you pull it.

2 Cut notches on each side at the head and foot
   of the bow, 5 cm (2 in) from each end. Cut them just
   deep enough to hold the bowstring so it
   doesn't slip.

3 Attach the bowstring to one notched end with a
   good all-around knot like the clove hitch (see page
   95). Tie a bowline (see page 94) in the other end of
   the string to make a small loop.

4 Now comes the tricky part. Brace the tied end of the bow
   against your foot, and hold the other end of the stick
   and the string loop in each hand. Pull the bow down, then slip
   your bowline loop over the end and into the notches.

How to shoot an arrow

1 Take your arrow and place in the bow, with the end of
   the arrow notched onto the bowstring.

2 Hold the bow up in front of you and look down the
   length of the arrow at your target.

3 Draw the bowstring back to your ear, keeping the
   arrow steady along the bow with your thumb.

4 Release the bowstring and the arrow, and watch
   the arrow sail off into the air.

A bow and arrow is a lethal weapon – even though the sticks you will be making don't have arrowheads, they can still cause injuries. Make sure to explain the points of safety to your children so that they understand they should never point it at a person, and always set up the target away from other people.

Ventriloquism

'Read my lips' just won't mean the same thing when you can throw your voice. While people do spend years getting really good at it, basic ventriloquism is actually surprisingly easy to grasp.

The goal, obviously, is to speak without moving your lips. But this doesn't mean with your mouth shut. The trick is to lock your jaws only slightly open, in a comfortable but unobtrusive fashion with the lips just slightly apart. This will let you speak without appearing to.

Some of the sounds we normally make when we talk require us to move our lips, so you'll have to learn how to make these sounds in a slightly different way. The letters that cause the most trouble are B, F, M, P and V. For B, try substituting a G sound, so that boys become goys and bank, gank. For F breathe hard as you say it and try for a sort of H sound. So Fred becomes Fhred. For M try N or Ng, substitute a K for any Ps (which doesn't sound as odd as you might think), and with a V try breathing out hard as you say it.

Practice makes perfect

Above all, practice. This probably won't be something that you find you have a natural talent for; you'll have to work at it a bit. Stand in front of the mirror, and run through the alphabet again and again. You don't want to give anything away, so this is best done in the restrooms at work. Repair there three or four times a day and recite the alphabet. Who could possibly mind? Then move on to words.

Choosing a dummy

Of course, once you have gained the ability to throw your voice, you need somewhere, so to speak, to toss it. This need not require anything elaborate. Kettles and pots – anything with a lid, really – can be made to talk by raising and lowering the lid. You can rig a dummy by drawing an eye on both sides of the first joint of your index finger, and putting a nice pair of red lips around the opening created by this finger and your thumb. Use one of your children's favourite toys, or wrap a dishtowel or other cloth around your forearm, cradle it in your other arm, and you have a talking baby.

Or you can use a human volunteer. Hoisting a child on to your knees, announce that you are going to make her talk. Whenever you tap her on the back, she opens and shuts her mouth, while you make the words come out of her. Any shortcomings in skill will be overlooked in the ensuing heightened hilarity.

Resist the temptation to make her say what you want to hear and go easy on lines like 'I will eat all my vegetables' and 'I will never whine at bedtime'. This is meant to be her entertainment, not your wish-fulfillment.

Juggling

Juggling is lots of fun and a great way to impress your youngsters, and it can keep them entertained for hours. When they get bored of watching you (as if they could!), start teaching them the simple beginner steps. If you can get them to master this simple method, you'll practically have your own family circus.

If you're completely new to juggling, it can be difficult to start, so build up in stages. Here are some exercises to get you going, starting with some simple beginner steps which are especially good to start children off with if they haven't completely mastered hand-eye coordination yet. One good tip is to start by throwing the balls higher than you normally would, to get an idea of what the pattern is like.

You will need
- ❖ 3 round, light objects of equal size, or professionally made juggling balls

Beginner

1 Hold two balls in your right hand and one in your left. Throw one ball from your right hand and catch it in the left.
2 Throw the ball back from your left hand and catch it in your right. Easy so far, right?
3 Practise until you never drop any of the balls. When you're feeling confident, move onto the next stage.

Intermediate

1   Again, start with two balls held in your right hand and one ball held in your left.
2   Throw one ball from your right hand as you did for the beginner's practice. As it reaches the top of its arc, throw the ball in your left hand.
3   Catch the first ball you threw in your left hand, and the second ball you threw in your right hand. The two balls should have exchanged places.
4   Again, practise this until you can do it without ever dropping a ball.

Advanced

1   Put two balls in your right hand and one in your left.
2   Start by throwing one of the balls in your right hand up and slightly to the left.
3   Then throw the ball in your left hand up and under the ball you just threw, as you did in the intermediate practice.
4   As you catch the first ball in your left hand throw the last ball in the air and catch the second ball with your right hand.
5   You are essentially playing catch with all three balls at the same time, so there's always a third ball in the air.
6   This can be pretty difficult to start with, so keep practising – count the number of throws you can manage before dropping any of the balls, to see how well you're doing. Gradually build up speed as you gain more control, and soon you'll be juggling like a professional.

Skimming stones

Skimming stones is a skill that will never fail to impress your children. Assuming you can make it skip more than once of course. The key to skimming stones is the stone itself. The ideal skimming stone is a flat, oblong-shaped one with round edges. Perfectly round ones are good, but oblong ones give you a place to put your index finger to ensure the right spin. Before you start, make sure your child knows she must never skim stones in an area where there are swimmers. Skimmed stones can sometimes move erratically, and nobody likes a stone in the head.

1 Position the rock in your hand so that your thumb is on top of the rock, your index finger is wrapped around the front edge, and your middle and ring fingers are stabilising it underneath.

2 Stand sideways to the water and pull your arm back, keeping the flat side of the rock parallel to the water.

3 Fling the rock with a side-arm motion. Bend your knees so you get low to the ground. You want the rock to hit the water at as low an angle as possible. Let the rock spin out of your hand and off the end of your index finger so that it spins horizontally, like a Frisbee landing on the water.

4 The harder your first throw is, the more the stone will 'take off' after the first skip. This can be fun, but it can also limit any further skims. Practise to get the speed of throw just right so your stone skips several times.

Making a kite

Reach up to the skies with a home-made kite. This can be quite fiddly, so an extra pair of hands is probably a good idea. With a bit of help you can build a great kite in about 45 minutes.

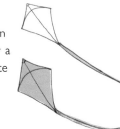

You will need

- ❖ One straight, thin piece of cane about 90 cm (3 ft) long
- ❖ One straight, thin piece of cane 45 cm (18 in) long
- ❖ A length of thick twine
- ❖ A long kite string
- ❖ A large piece of thick white paper, at least 90 x 30 cm (3 x 1 ft)
- ❖ Scissors
- ❖ Masking tape
- ❖ Ribbon

1 Cut thin, shallow notches in the ends of both lengths of cane. These notches don't have to be thicker than the blade of the knife.
2 Make a cross by placing the shorter piece of cane over the longer piece. They should intersect about a foot down on the longer piece.
3 Secure them in place by lashing them with thick twine. Pass the twine round the crossing point in an 'X', and tuck the end under the loops to finish off.
4 Now make a tight frame of twine around the canes, using the notches you made in step 1 as guides. First make a loop in the end of the twine, using a bowline knot (see page 94). Lodge the knot on one notch (so the loop hangs free the other side) and stretch the string all the way around, passing through each notch until you come back to the loop.

5 Pass the twine through the loop and stretch it back round the frame in the reverse direction. Repeat steps 4 and 5 a few times. This will make the twine frame taut. Be careful not to make it too tight or the canes will warp.

6 Lay the cane and twine frame over your sheet of paper. Trace around the kite frame onto the paper, giving yourself at least 2.5 cm (1 in) extra paper all around the outline.

7 Cut the shape of the kite out of the paper. Don't forget to make the paper a little larger than the kite. Attach the paper to the face of the cane kite frame by folding the extra width of paper over the twine all the way around, and taping it to the back.

8 Create the kite 'harness' by tying a piece of twine at the top and bottom of the long piece of cane, and another piece at the ends of the shorter piece of cane. They should intersect about 15 cm (6 in) above the intersection of the canes. Tie the two pieces of twine together at that point, and make a small twine loop in one of the tied ends. This is where you'll attach your kite string when you're ready to fly.

9 Make a kite tail with a 90cm (3ft) length of twine. Tie 10cm (4in) pieces of ribbon to the twine every 15 cm (6in) or so as decoration.

10 Tie the kite string to the loop, and you're ready to take your kite outside on a windy day and launch! You can fly your kite as is, or you can colour or paint it however you like.

Make sure your decoration is even so that your kite stays balanced – if you have too much weight on one side, the kite will spin out of control when the wind blows and crash rather than fly. Getting the tail right is also key – if it is too short, the kite will be unbalanced, while a long tail may add too much weight.

Pick a card

This is a basic card trick that will impress any audience, even adults. You hold in your hand a deck of cards. Fan them out, shuffle them, fire them from one hand to the other, whatever. Ask a member of the audience to take a card. Have them look at it, and tell them to make sure that you don't see it. Have them show it to the other members of the audience. Then tell them to put it back on the top of the deck. Cut the cards once, maybe even a couple of times, pass your hands over the deck in a mysterious fashion, say some appropriate magic words, and then turn the cards over so you can see their faces, and fan them out. Then pull out their card and show it to them.

The magician's secret

This classic card trick is really quite simple. The secret lies in what magicians call the key card. At some point – before you begin the trick, while you are performing your preliminary mumbo jumbo or as you are holding the cards out to your volunteer – sneak a look at the bottom card. This will be your key card. You don't have to be too discreet about sneaking a peek, especially if you can distract your audience at the same time. When you cut the cards, your key card will end up on top of their card. When you flip the cards over, their card will be to the left of your key card. Once you spot it, you know which card is theirs.

The key card need not always be the bottom card. The top card will work just as well – just remember their card will come after it when you fan them out, not before. And once you gain a bit of practice you can even try cutting the cards a couple of times – but be careful – or employing the Hindu shuffle.

The Hindu shuffle

Here is how this shuffle works. Once your volunteer has put their card on top of the deck, you pick up the pack in your right hand, and drop the top few cards into your left hand. Then you begin to shuffle by dropping more small packets of cards into your left hand – but always behind the first cards you dropped in there. This goes on until there are only a few cards left in your right hand, including your key card. This packet you drop in front of all the other cards in your left hand. The key card is now on top of their pick. Turn the cards over, work your way through, find your key card and lift out their card – the one on its left.

Work at this one solo for a while before debuting it: finding your key card, picking a card out, returning it and making sure you can find it. When it comes to performing, create some distracting stage patter, to give you a better chance of seeing your key card unobtrusively.

Making a hovercraft

If your child should happen to ask you how a hovercraft works (children are naturally inquisitive creatures and are likely to ask you all manner of questions that you don't know the answer to), with this entertaining actvity, you can not only tell them how it works, you can show them as you build one together.

Hovercrafts use huge fans to create an air cushion between themselves and the land or water underneath, so that they can glide over the top of any surface. Because they hardly touch the terrain they're travelling over, hovercraft experience very little friction. This means that they can reach impressive speeds: the world record is 137 kmph (85 mph). But for the same reason they can be pretty hard to steer, skidding round corners, especially at high speeds. And they don't have any brakes. You stop one by letting down the cushion of air so the craft comes to rest. That's one reason why you don't see a lot of hovercraft out on the roads.

Nevertheless, enthusiasts around the world build and race small hovercraft, mostly built to hold just one person. This tabletop model is a little less ambitious. All you need are a few household items.

You will need
- ❖ An old CD
- ❖ A pull-up water-bottle lid
- ❖ Glue
- ❖ A balloon
- ❖ A table top

1 Glue the water bottle lid over the centre hole of the old CD and let it sit until it's dry – this might take a few hours, so leave it overnight. Make sure the glue goes all the way round the bottle lid, so that air can't escape at the edges.

2   When the glue has dried, pull up the bottle lid as if you're going to take a drink of water.

3   Blow up the balloon all the way and pinch the neck to prevent air from getting out. (Don't tie it off, though, since you're going to want to let the air out any moment.)

4   While still holding the balloon closed, pull the rim of the balloon neck over the bottle top so it makes a good seal. Then set the CD down on a flat surface – a table top or polished floor works great.

5   Let go of the balloon so the air can come out through the bottle top. The CD should lift off the table! Give it a gentle push and watch it glide.

6   Just like a real hovercraft, a cushion of air is being forced under the CD (from the pressure inside the balloon) that allows it to levitate off the ground. Because the bottom of the CD is pushed away from the surface of the table, it can glide along for quite a distance, at least until the air in the balloon runs out.

7   However, unlike a real hovercraft, your homemade model doesn't have a skirt to hold the air in and maintain the high pressure. This means it runs down a lot quicker, and it's also less stable where the surface it's travelling over isn't smooth and firm. You can try getting it to work on a flat pool of water, but you might well find your CD just flips over.

Balloon animals

Here is an amusement that punches far above its weight. Learn this one and you'll be more than a father-entertainer; you'll have attained the status of mega-Dad. Balloon animals need long, skinny latex balloons available in joke stores, party supply shops and probably in toy departments elsewhere. (On a green note, they are fully bio-degradable, too.) When you go to buy them, just explain what you need them for. A caution: these balloons are a little heavier than conventional balloons, so unless you have the lungs of a Sherpa raised in the foothills of the Himalayas, you'll need a source of air. This can be an electric pump but a bicycle pump or similar hand pump will work just as well. Just hold the balloon over the nozzle – you don't need that good a seal – and fill them up.

There isn't really a secret to creating balloon animals. All you need to know is how to bend the balloon in different directions, using these twists in the balloon to create different shapes. Let's take a look at the dog, the basic balloon animal.

1   Take one of your balloons and inflate it, leaving about 7.5 cm (3 in) uninflated at the end – you'll need this slack. Knot the mouth of the balloon.
2   From the knotted end, first measure down roughly 7.5 cm (3 in) and make a twist in the balloon. What you have here (let's call it a link, like in a sausage), is your dog's head. For the moment, don't let go, because it will unwind.

3   Now measure down a further 7.5 cm (3 in), and make another twist. That's one of his ears. Fold these two links down, so that they run along the side of the balloon, then measure off a third link – his other ear – and give it a twist.

4   When you have done this, take your first link, and bend it across the balloon, so that the twist between the first and the second link overlaps the twist between the third link and the rest of the balloon. Twist the first link around this link twice. This is called locking, and it means the twists won't come loose. You now have the dog's head and ears.

5   Now measure down the balloon another 7.5 cm (3 in), and make a twist. This is his neck. After this make another twist, followed by another one. These are his front legs. Bend the third link up so it is beside the second link, and twist the last joint around the neck joint, locking it. You now have the neck, the front legs and a long, unformed body.

6   Measure off a few more inches and twist to seal off the body link, then make two more twists (are we thinking dachshund or beagle?) as before, creating two more links that will become the rear legs. Fold up at the joint between the legs and twist the last joint twice around the hip joint, to make his tail. You have inflatable canine perfection.

Once you get the basics of twisting and locking, you can move on to other animals: giraffe (make the neck longer), rabbits (boost the ears, and then boost the hind legs and tuck them under the body), and so on. Let imagination and experimentation be your guides.

The mind reader

The mind-reading dad successfully guesses any number between one and 10. 'I am Number-oh, the mind reader', you announce to your audience, in a suitably portentous voice. 'I want you to think of a number between one and 10. But don't tell me what it is.'

With the number securely recorded in your audience's mind, you then ask them to put it through the following contortions, without telling you any of the results.

1 Multiply the number by three.
2 Add one to the result.
3 Multiply that number by three.
4 Now add the original number.

A pen and paper, or electronic calculator may be required for younger, or less mathematically gifted children. With these four steps completed, you ask them for the result of their calculation. All being well, this should be a double-digit number. You simply need to strike off the second digit and you will be left with the original number.

This is a variant on the trick that many 'mind readers' use to figure out a person's age, although modified a little here. Firstly, for the good reason that you really ought to know your children's ages already, so they are unlikely to be terribly impressed if you manage to guess them. Secondly, if you are the sort of father who needs a trick to learn how old his children are, then you are probably not the sort of father who spends a great deal of time entertaining them in the first place. If indeed you even know where they are.

Creating a flip book

This is not so much a trick to show off, as a skill to teach. (It was, I believe, the venerable sage Confucius who said, 'Make a child a flip book and you amuse her for about ten seconds; teach a child to make them and amuse her for, if not a lifetime, certainly rather longer.') And as making flip books can be somewhat time-consuming, after you impart your knowledge you will be free to nap, watch TV and undertake other such important activities.

1   The first thing you'll need is a supply of light card. Classic index cards would be a good choice, but if you can't find them any quantity of equally flimsy cardstock would work fine. With index cards, start by cutting them widthwise to make strips about 2.5 cm (1 in) across. You should be able to get five such strips out of one index card.

2   To make things easier, start with just a stick figure running for your first attempt. On the first index-card strip, draw a stick figure with his legs wide apart as if he were belting along.

3   Then move this strip up, and use our man as a reference for the second strip, where you show your character with his legs in a slightly different spot.

4   Move up the second strip and use the newly positioned character as a reference while you make the third, and on and on.

5   When you have a bunch of these, gather them up, make sure that the outer edges of your card pieces (on the side of the image) are more or less even for ease of riffling, and clip the lot together at the other end with a paper or bulldog clip. Now flick through the pages with your thumb and behold – Dad is a regular Martin Scorsese.

Story time

Whether it's a Sunday afternoon ritual or just before bedtime, reading stories to your children is one of the most rewarding 'duties' of fatherhood. You can see the little imaginations working overtime as they enter a new world – and Dad is holding the door open!

Getting them interested

Start reading to them when they're young. Listening is something they'll be doing all through school, so it's never too soon to introduce them. When they're a bit older, let them help choose the stories as well. Once you've got through their favorites, go to the bookshop or even better the library and find some new ones

Don't feel you have to use funny voices – unless you want to! Just read slowly and clearly and their active imaginations will do the rest. Above all, know when to stop. Kids have a shorter attention span than dads, so keep it short and sweet.

Suggested stories for pre-schoolers

- *The Very Hungry Caterpillar* – Eric Carle
- *The Bad-tempered Ladybird* by the same author
- *James and the Giant Peach* – Roald Dahl wrote this as long ago as 1961 but it's truly timeless
- *How Do Dinosaurs Say Good Night* – Jane Yolen. Its companion volume is *How Do Dinosaurs Eat their Food?*
- *Green Eggs and Ham* – one of many Dr. Seuss classics
- *The Moon* – Robert Louis Stevenson's classic poem, beautifully illustrated, became a sweet bedtime book.

Three-coin football

This two-player tabletop pastime, also known as penny football or coin football, is much more fun than many board games. You need three coins of identical size, a flat table with a smooth surface and a steady hand. If you're anything like this Dad, small change is probably all you have, so be thankful for small mercies!

The rules

After tossing a coin to decide who starts, Player 1 places the three coins in a triangular formation, with all coins touching. Player 2 makes a goal on the opposite edge of the table by placing her little and index fingers flat on the surface. Each finger is a goalpost.

Player 1 scatters the pennies by flicking one, and continues in play unless a coin falls off the table or there is a foul. For a goal to be scored, the 'ball' must be flicked not only between the goalposts but must pass between the other two coins on the table – otherwise it does not count.

A foul occurs when two of the attacker's coins collide (except from the kick-off) or she pushes the coin in an irregular manner, e.g. hits it twice in succession.

After a foul or a goal, Player 2 becomes the attacker and must try to score in Player 1's goal in a similar way. The game continues up to a pre-determined time or up to a designated number of goals.

Musical chairs

The game of musical chairs is as old as the hills but still a favourite game to entertain a group of chldren. You need the same number of chairs as children. Have the children dance round the chairs in a circular fashion then take one of the chairs away while the music is playing. Once the music stops, everyone tries to get their backside on a chair – and someone will miss out.

You, as the man in charge, will have to come up with the music and adjudicate in the event of disagreements, which happen pretty often. You can spice it up by making people dress up, make losers pay a forfeit or spreading the chairs out over a larger area.

Blow football

Long before computer games, Subbuteo and even those tables with men on a metal rod, our grandfathers were playing blow football with our dads. You can, too, with your sons (and daughters).

All you need are some large drinking straws, a ping-pong ball and a couple of goals. Margarine tubs are particularly good. Some people use a (relatively flat) table, others the carpet – in which case use books to mark out the pitch extent.

The first to an agreed amount of goals – five, usually – is the winner. The ball is only to be propelled by breath and if anything else touches it a penalty is given. This means the team offended against gets the chance to score unopposed, and the fouler cannot pick up their straw until the first puff has been made.

Thumb wars

Also known as thumb wrestling, this is a game played with two players, often in situations where larger or more complicated games are impossible – such as in the car, a restaurant or school.

Players make a fist with four fingers of one hand together and thrust it towards their opponent, who reciprocates. Battle will be entered after a chant: 'One, two, three, four, I declare a thumb war; five, six, seven, eight, try to keep your thumb straight. Nine, ten, let's begin.' The opponents then proceed to attempt to pin (capture or trap) their opponent's thumb for five seconds while avoiding the same fate. Victory is hailed with the chant '1, 2, 3, 4, I won a thumb war!' Look out for sneak attacks with index fingers.

Penny up the wall

Both players stand the same distance from a wall and throw or flick (never roll) their penny at it, aiming to get as close as the bottom of the wall as possible. The person whose coin is adjudged closest to the wall wins them all.

There are various variations including that 'standers' (coins that balance upright on their end) pay double. Another, more anarchic game called Scramble involves throwing a handful of low-value coins on the ground, shouting 'scramble' and watching the carnage commence. It's not recommended to play with coins of high denominations unless you're feeling particularly affluent that day. High stakes can magnify disagreements.

Adventurous Dad

- Building a treehouse
- Making a compass
- Growing a sunflower
- Tying knots
- Creating a bottle rocket

The great outdoors is nature's playground, and dads can recall enjoying every inch of freedom they were allowed as kids. Now it's your turn to guide your own offspring through the challenges of putting up tents, observing insects, birds and animals and tying knots. With all these suggestions you can get your children out of the house, away from the television and introduce them to all the fun that can be had in the great outdoors.

Building a treehouse

Building a treehouse is a must for an adventurous outdoors dad. It will provide your children with endless outdoors entertainment, as a look-out platform, fort or base camp.

Finding the right tree to build in is the key to a sturdy treehouse. Choose one with a minimum of three branches that spread out equal distances from one side of the trunk. They should be at least 20 cm (8 in) thick to support the weight of your child and a few of his friends. Don't build it too high up – a treehouse platform acts a bit like a sail when it comes to the wind and things can sway around a lot. Better to aim for between 3 and 4.5 m (10 and 15 ft) off the ground. That'll still feel quite high enough in a breeze!

You will need
- ❖ A tree
- ❖ Several lengths of wood, 5 x 10 cm (2 x 4 in)
- ❖ A saw
- ❖ 5-cm (2-in) galvanised nails
- ❖ A hammer
- ❖ A sheet of 2-cm (1-in) thick plywood, 1.2 x 2.4 m (4 x 8 ft)
- ❖ A ladder
- ❖ Rope

1 Start by cutting 45-cm (18-in) long pieces from your lengths of wood to make a basic ladder up the trunk of the tree. Pick the exact spot you want to build in, and work out how many rungs you'll need on the ladder to climb up to it.

2 Once the lengths have been cut, use at least two nails set side-by-side in each piece to nail the rungs to the tree. Space them about 60 cm (2 ft) apart, leading up the trunk to the base of the branches where the platform of the treehouse will be secured.

3 How you access the platform will depend on the shape of your tree. Most of the time, the ladder will come up right under the best branches for building on. That's fine: you'll just have to cut a hole in the floor to climb through. If you keep the piece of wood you cut out, you can use it to make a trap door.

4 Next, haul the sheet of plywood into the tree and position it between the branches where you think it will be most sturdy.

5 Mark the tree limbs with a pencil or nail where the plywood touches them and lower the plywood back down.

6 Cut several more 45-cm (18-in) long pieces of wood and nail them to the tree where you've marked to act as blocks for the platform.

7 Lift the plywood carefully into place by having two people on the ground pass it up to two people in the tree. Nail the plywood to the blocks.

8 Next, make railings by nailing up more lengths of plywood between the branches or by tying up lengths of rope to surround the platform.

9 From here you can add a trap door, extra ladder steps leading to higher branches, and miniature seats or platforms on surrounding look-out points.

Essential kit for outdoor Dad

The great outdoors is both inspiring and scary. Make it less scary for yourself by taking the following with you on any adventurous day out.

- ❖ Wellies/stout boots. Work from the ground up and keep yourself dry and comfortable.
- ❖ Rainproof jackets. You never can tell what the weather might do next. It might look bright and sunny, the weatherman might promise a dry day, but you're always better safe than sorry!
- ❖ Pocket knife or multi-purpose tool. You never know when this will come in handy – but keep blades away from your children.
- ❖ First aid kit (including blister treatment). Don't let an assortment of minor injuries – cuts, scrapes, nettle stings – spoil your day.
- ❖ Wet wipes – for use at either end – oh, and a roll of toilet paper could be well worth the space it takes up in your bag.
- ❖ Map and compass. If you're not going to stop and ask for directions, at least equip yourself with the means to find your own way.
- ❖ Flashlight. Just in case the outing lasts a little longer than scheduled.
- ❖ Drinks bottle(s). It's always important to stay hydrated when out and about.
- ❖ Sun/rain protection. Hats, sunscreen and umbrellas will mean you have most bases covered for whatever the weather decides to do.
- ❖ Trail snacks. Fruit and nut bars will give quick energy when spirits flag and bodies start to tire.
- ❖ Mobile phone. For when all else fails!

When venturing into the great outdoors, it is important to make sure you are prepared for any eventuality, but you should also bear in mind how much weight you will have to carry. Overloading yourself with kit will only cause further problems. Decide what is really necessary, and where possible try to take handy travel-size packets with you.

Making a tent

You can't conquer the great outdoors without a camping trip, and you can't go camping without a tent. Well, not comfortably anyway. You can of course buy a tent, but if you really want to prove your status as an outdoorsman, you can make your own.

You will need
- ❖ A 2.4 x 3.6 m (8 x 12 ft) tarpaulin with grommets (eye-holes) round the edges
- ❖ 7 m (24 ft) of rope
- ❖ At least four large rocks, stakes or sticks

1 Locate two trees about 3 m (10 ft) apart. These will act as the supports for your tent.
2 Run your rope through the centre grommet on each of the longer sides of the tarpaulin, bisecting it into 1.3 x 2.4 m (6 x 8 ft) rectangles.
3 About 1.5 m (5 ft) off the ground, securely tie your rope to the trees you've selected. The point of tie-off should be roughly the same height on each tree. The tarpaulin should drape over this roof-line to form a tent.
4 Use large rocks, stakes or sticks to secure the corners of the tarpaulin, making sure to stretch the sides of your tent taut. Now you're ready to camp!

Pitching a tent

A child's first experience of life under canvas is
inevitably in the safe confines of the back garden. But
putting up a tent, no matter where, can rob even
the most confident dad of his aura of omniscience.
Stop and think about the task before rushing in, tent poles blazing…

1   First, check all the pieces are there. A mallet is very important, and
    often missing or not supplied!
2   Choose a suitable level patch of grass, away from any hazards, and
    clear it of sticks and stones. Lay out your groundsheet in position
    and weigh corners to ensure it stays put.
3   Peg the tent out, putting a peg through each loop at the tent
    corners. Ensure the canvas is stretched tight as you do so – sagging
    tents are amazingly unimpressive.
4   Stick the pole pieces together in the right order. Not as easy as you
    think. If in doubt, check it out.
5   Insert the main tent pole into the hole in the canvas, and ensure it
    stays upright by attaching guy ropes. Then erect the other pole(s),
    pulling guy ropes as far as possible from the tent for maximum
    tension. Hammer the pegs at 45-degree angles, blunt end facing
    away from the tent, so it's hard for the wind to pull them out
6   Cover with a fly sheet to make it extra rain proof.
7   Invite children into your newly built domain.

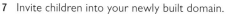

Learning to ride a bike

Learning to ride a two-wheeler unaided is a milestone
in any child's life and no dad would want to miss it.
Here are some hints to maximise the pride and minimise
the pain.

- ❖ Tuition should be done in a flat space, such
  as an empty parking lot, a field with short,
  hard-packed grass or a path surrounded by grass.
- ❖ Make sure the bike is the right size for your child. If in doubt,
  borrow a smaller one to give him added confidence.
- ❖ Buy a suitably sized helmet and make sure your child wears it
  every time he rides. Also consider protective clothing like knee
  pads, or at the least sturdy jeans and jacket.
- ❖ Explain the importance of biking in safe locations.
- ❖ Discuss what to do if he falls, and explain that this is part of the
  learning process.
- ❖ Remove the training wheels only at the appropriate time and
  with your child's agreement.
- ❖ Run along behind, holding him by the shoulders. Don't hold
  onto the saddle or any other part of the bike, as he won't
  realise he is leaning to one side or the other. If you hold him by
  the shoulders, he will feel the pressure as he leans to the side
  and learn to reduce it.
- ❖ Do not make any attempt to steer your child; let him feel in
  control. If running along holding his shoulders is too difficult, an
  alternative is to lash a stick to the back of the saddle between
  the seat stays and use it as a handle.

Repairing a bicycle puncture

If you thought it was all over when you taught him to ride a bike think again! To get your child back in the saddle you'll need a puncture repair kit, some tyre levers (or similar) and plenty of Dad's most precious resource – patience.

1 Remove the wheel from the frame. Use a tyre lever (or, if unavailable, a screwdriver) to prise the tyre off the wheel.
2 Starting opposite the valve, pull the inner tube out of the tyre, keeping it near the corresponding part of the tyre so that you can find what caused the puncture.
3 Inflate the tube, listening for the hiss of escaping air – this is easier than spotting it by eye. If you can't find it, remove the tube entirely, submerge it in water, and look for the bubbles of escaping air.
4 When you find the puncture, scrape the area around it to roughen the rubber. Cover the area with cement (from the patch kit) and wait five minutes for the cement to dry.
5 While the cement is drying, find and remove the object that caused the puncture. If there is a gash in the tyre, place a fabric square between the tube and the tyre to avoid another puncture.
6 When the cement is dry, peel the silver foil off the patch and apply that side to the tyre. Rub hard from the centre toward the edges so that it sticks well. Inflate the inner tube slightly and pack it back into the tyre, then squeeze the tyre back within the rim of the wheel.
7 Before fully inflating the tube, put the wheel back onto the bicycle, then inflate it to the same pressure as the other tyre.

Building a raft

You can build a raft in a weekend if you have all the right materials, including the right-sized logs. Recruit some family help to find the logs and fit them all together. If possible, build it close to the water so that you can easily push the raft in when you've finished, rather than having to drag it down to the river first.

You will need
- A knife
- A saw
- An axe
- Rope
- About 20 logs, 2 m (6 ft) long and 15 cm (6 in) in diameter

1 Find some fallen trees, or if you're feeling energetic, saw or chop down some trees. You're looking for mid-size trees, roughly 15 cm (6 in) in diameter (a bit fatter than your leg) and about 2 m (6 ft) long. This is going to be a square raft 2 m (6 ft) long on each side.

2 Make a square with four logs, using an axe to make notches at each end so that they fit together where they overlap.

3 Lash the logs together with rope at the corners using a clove hitch knot (see page 95) to secure them in place.

4 Make the deck by notching more logs to fit and laying them across the square. Lash them all in place. The deck logs shouldn't be too close to each other because you'll need room for the lashing.

5 Lay two more logs across the tops of the ends of the deck logs and lash these into place to hold your deck together. Drag your raft to the water and launch!

Whenever you take your children near water, safety should come first. So when you take your children on your raft, make sure everyone wears a life jacket (and you should lead by example), even if everyone knows how to swim and the water appears to be fairly calm and shallow.

Make a compass

When a dad goes adventuring, he should always take a compass to help him find his way home if he strays too far and needs to get the children back in time for bed. Unfortunately, there are times you may forget to pack a real compass, accidentally drop it off a hillside, or give it to your child to look after who promptly leaves it at the next rest stop. No worries – you can make one. Fortunately, the Earth's magnetic field is strong enough to attract magnetised sewing needles or paper clips, if they're given freedom to spin by being floated on water. Here's how to set up your own so you can always tell which way is north. (This method won't work if you use a bowl made from ferrous metal to hold the water. The magnetised needle will be attracted to the metal bowl instead of swinging freely to point north.)

You will need
- ❖ A magnet
- ❖ A container to hold water
- ❖ Water
- ❖ A leaf or large blade of grass
- ❖ A small piece of metal, like a needle, paperclip or small nail

1 Run the magnet slowly over the needle about 10 times, in the same direction each time. This will make the needle magnetic enough to act as a compass.
2 If you don't have a magnet you can still magnetise your needle or paper clip using static electricity. You can use material from a nylon raincoat or fleece jacket to build up the charge. Simply stroke the needle in the same direction with the material you have on hand. Do this at least 50 times.

3 Fill a container with water and gently place a leaf or large blade of grass so it floats on top of the water in the centre of the container.

4 Carefully place the magnetised needle on top of the floating leaf or grass, so it floats freely on the surface of the water.

5 Watch as the needle turns to point itself towards the North Pole.

6 Try to test your home-made compass in a place that's sheltered from the wind. Earth's magnetic poles might be strong enough to attract a magnetised needle but that's not saying much. A breeze, even a gentle one, can easily push your leaf off course.

7 Of course, this will only show you a line between north and south. You need some other clues to work out which is which. The sun is one clue: in the northern hemisphere, the sun will always be in the southern half of the sky, on the eastern side in the morning and the western side in the evening. In the southern hemisphere, the sun will always be on the northern side of the sky.

Build a sundial

You can also use your home-made compass to help tell the time. But first you have to build a sundial. Sundials are the world's oldest clocks – they work on the simple principle that the sun is always in the same direction at noon: directly south in the northern hemisphere, and directly north in the southern hemisphere. (At noon on the Equator, in case you were wondering, the sun is always directly overhead.)

By making your own sundial, you can tell time using the sun and the shadows it creates. Constructing the device takes about 10 minutes, but marking the clock face takes several hours – from 9 am to 3 pm – as the sun moves across the sky.

You will need
- ❖ A shoebox
- ❖ A screwdriver
- ❖ A straight stick – a bamboo cane works well
- ❖ Masking tape
- ❖ A black marker
- ❖ A compass
- ❖ A full sunny day

1 Turn the shoebox upright. Draw a circle in the middle of one end.
2 Using a screwdriver, poke a hole in the middle of the circle. Then poke a hole in the bottom of the shoebox below the first hole, but a little further back.
3 Push your stick through the first hole and angle it back towards the end of the shoebox. Push the tip of the stick through the second hole you made and tape it in place. Your stick should now be firmly held so it pokes up at an angle out of the circle on the top of the box.

4   Take your sundial outside and place it on a flat surface out in the open where it won't be disturbed. If you need to steady it against the wind, you can put a large stone or brick in the bottom of the shoebox to weigh it down.

5   Use a compass to find north, and point the stick in that direction if you're in the northern hemisphere, or south if you're in the southern hemisphere. The stick should throw a good, clear shadow across the circle you drew.

6   At exactly 9 am, draw a line marking the position of the shadow of the stick on the circle you drew in step 1. Mark it with a straight line and label it 9 am.

7   Each hour after that, revisit your sundial and mark the new location of the shadow with 10 am, 11 am, 12 noon, 1 pm, 2 pm and 3 pm. Your sundial is now ready to tell the time. If you want your sundial to work before 9 am, you have to get up early and mark the shadow exactly on the hour. If you want it to work later, keep marking the shadow on the hour until the sun goes down.

8   Whenever you want to use the sundial, take it outside and use your compass to point the stick in the right direction, as you did in step 5. Then see where the shadow falls in relation to the lines you've already drawn.

9   Remember that if your local time changes by an hour from winter into summer, your sundial will only be correct for the time of year when you set it up.

Set up a bird table

Birds are true wonders of nature – and there's so much fun to be had by observing them at close quarters. Dad's woodworking skills can help make this reality.

A bird table will attract them to your window and give you the best seat in the (bird)house! The good news is a bird table does not need to be fancy or complicated – the birds just want a good supply of food served up in a safe, sheltered place. A bird table is most valuable in winter, from October to April when natural food is in short supply. At the end of the season the appearance of large numbers of insects and the buds on the trees starting to open tell you that you can now stop feeding.

The table can be left in position all year round, but bringing it in out of the weather during the summer will probably prolong its life. It's okay to continue feeding birds during the spring and summer as long as hard foods are avoided; these can be a danger to fledglings if a bird takes the food back to its nest.

If it takes a few days before you see any birds, don't be discouraged. Once they discover the food and convince themselves it's not a cunning trap, they will visit regularly.

Choosing materials

A cheap piece of solid timber makes an excellent bird table, but use wood that will not split or disintegrate when wet – exterior quality plywood 0.5 to 1 cm thick is ideal. Sand the wood smooth to remove crevices that can hold dirt and disease. It is best to leave the table untreated. If it must be treated to prolong its life, use a water-based preservative and make sure it is dry before use.

There's no maximum size, but don't make the table too small or the birds will squabble and the shyer species kept away: 30 by 50 cm is about right. A rim 1 cm high around the edge will help stop food from being knocked or blown off – but leave gaps at the corners to allow rain to drain away and make cleaning easy.

A roof provides a dry place for seed hoppers and nut containers and gives some protection from rain, snow and sparrowhawks. Some birds may even roost at night on a table with a roof. But this can deter the shyer and larger species from visiting so, in most cases, an open table is just as good.

Make sure your bird table is inaccessible to cats or squirrels: put it 1 to 2 metres above the ground and make it hard for any animal to climb up. Plastic piping is a good countermeasure. Alternatively hang the table from a branch or clothes line, or mount on a window ledge with brackets. Above all, make sure it's somewhere quiet and sheltered.

Put out some bird feed on the table and wait to see who shows up. You could also strategically place a few nails or hooks in the edges of the table for hanging nut and seed feeders or fat balls.

Nature in the back yard

Most children are intrigued by creatures that live in your backyard – spiders, ladybugs, slugs, snails, woodlice and ants. Dads must overcome any natural feelings of revulsion and get down and dirty with the kids. There's a world of wildlife in your back garden – or, if you don't have one, your local park. You never know, you might enjoy it!

Under rocks

Check what should be around at certain times of the year, then go and search for them, in bushes or among flowers and grass, under rocks, underground or in ponds.

A useful item to have around is a 'bug box', a clear plastic cube with a magnifier in the lid that will make anything placed inside the box bigger. You also want equip your co-workers with a large pad and drawing materials, or even better an exercise book in which to record their finds. Most of what you find will be insects local to your home. With the help of a book, you can identify the insect and make a guess as to its habitat.

Even seasons

If you set up a quadrat or sampling area, you can get your children to examine it minutely and record exactly what they find. Then you can set up quadrats of the same size (say one square metre, the borders marked by pieces of wood or other material) in different places or different seasons of the year and compare your findings.

Grow a monster sunflower

Even dads without green fingers can give gardening a go – and this is the ideal starter project. Sunflowers are the showoffs of the horticultural world. They can grow to heights approaching ten feet, and their seeds are high in protein. Best of all, they're easy to grow!

- ❖ It's best to start them indoors, in small (three-inch) pots of peat or compost, putting a maximum of two or three seeds in a pot.
- ❖ Water the seeds well, but don't let your children over-water them!
- ❖ Keep them warm – some people use a covering of bubble wrap to encourage germination.
- ❖ May is a good time to transplant them from the window ledge to the outside world, when the frosts are definitely over and done with. Hopefully they will have developed decent-sized roots by this time and be able to fend for themselves.
- ❖ When you transplant sunflowers into your garden put them somewhere they will get regular sun. They will tend to face the east as that is where the sun comes up, so bear this in mind. But support may also be needed for those long stems, so up against a fence would be a good spot. Let the budding gardeners play their part in choosing where they should go and digging the holes. It could be the beginning of a lifelong hobby.

Tying knots

No dad should set off for a day of adventure without knowing how to tie a few good knots. If you ever want to try sailing or mountain climbing, knowing how to tie these knots will give you a head start. All you need is a piece of rope. Or string if you're just practising.

Reef knot

A reef knot is easy to tie, and can be used in most situations. It's also easy to loosen: just push one end towards the knot.

1 Using two ropes, make an 'X' left over right, and then bring one end through the loop as if you're tying your shoelaces.
2 Repeat this process, but this time make the 'X' right over left. Pull it tight, and you will have the knot.

Bowline

Rock climbers use the bowline because it forms a quick non-slipping loop – perfect for attaching yourself to a climbing buddy as you scale the side of a mountain or climb your favourite tree. It's known by some as 'the king of knots'.

1 Begin by making a loop in one end of the rope.
2 Then take the other end up through the loop, around the rope on the other side, and back where it came from.
3 In the Scouts, they used to teach it to young'uns with the old 'rabbit story': the rabbit comes up through the hole, round the tree, and back down the hole again.

Clove hitch

The clove hitch is the best knot to use when lashing two logs or pieces of wood together, to make a raft or treehouse. Not only is it easy on the rope, but because the rope crosses over on itself the knot actually gets stronger the harder you pull on it.

1 Make this knot by looping the rope over the log. Pass the end of the rope over and across itself and around the wood again.
2 Then feed the end under the rope crossing the top, so that it comes out in the opposite direction to the rest of the rope.

Timber hitch

If you find something big in the woods and want to drag it home you'll need to know the timber hitch. This is the knot that lumberjacks used to tie around fallen tree trunks to drag the timber to the saw mill.

1 Loop your rope around a log and bring the short end up and around the long end of the rope.
2 Bring the short end back down through the loop from the direction in which it came.
3 Bring it over and under itself two or three times. When the long end is pulled, the knot tightens onto itself.

Launching a bottle rocket

The pinnacle of adventurous experimentation has got to be launching a rocket into the air. You can delight and fascinate your children with the ability to make a bottle fly! One of the easiest rockets to make is known as a water or bottle rocket. By pressurising air inside a plastic bottle that has a little water in it, you can send the device flying surprisingly high into the air. The air pushes the water out of the bottle with enough force to launch it. The rocket takes about an hour to make.

You will need
- ❖ A large plastic bottle
- ❖ A rubber stopper with a small hole in its centre, which can fit snugly in the mouth of the bottle
- ❖ A 30-cm (1-ft) long straw 6 mm (¼ in) in diameter
- ❖ Clear plastic packing tape
- ❖ Scissors
- ❖ Sturdy cardboard
- ❖ A 30-cm (1-ft) metal or wooden rod just less than 6 mm (¼ in) in diameter
- ❖ Water
- ❖ A pump with a needle
- ❖ Plastic tubing to extend bicycle pump hose

To construct the rocket

1 Tape the straw to the exterior of the bottle. Make sure it is aligned with the centre of the bottle. You will use this to launch the rocket.
2 Cut four rocket fins out of cardboard and tape them to the outside of the bottle around the mouth. Be careful not to cover or

The amount of water in the bottle will determine how high or low the rocket will fly. If you put in too much water, it will make the bottle too heavy, but too little water means there won't be enough thrust. You may have to experiment with the water level a few times to get it right and make your device fly higher.

compress the straw. The rocket will launch upside-down, so the mouth of the bottle will be the bottom of the rocket.

3 Create a nose cone out of cardboard and tape it onto the top of the rocket (that is, the bottom of the bottle).

To launch the rocket

1 Fill the bottle up to about halfway with water.

2 Push the rubber stopper securely into the mouth of the bottle. Tape it down if need be to hold it in place, leaving the small hole at the centre of the stopper open. If you can't find a stopper with a hole, drill a hole through a wine-bottle cork and use that instead.

3 Fit a bicycle pump with about 3 m (10 ft) of extension tubing, fixing the pump needle at the end of the hose. If you don't have extension tubing, don't worry – just remember that whoever is pumping is going to get wet when the rocket takes off.

4 In a field, sink the rod straight into the ground and slide the straw taped to the side of the rocket onto it. Make sure the rocket is pointing directly upwards.

5 Push the needle through the hole in the rubber stopper.

6 Before launching the rocket, make sure that everyone is standing well back and that the rocket isn't pointing directly at anyone. Stand well back and pump air into the bottle at a steady rate.

7 When the pressure in the bottle gets high enough, the rocket will blast off in an explosion of water!

Make a snowman

The look on your child's face when they first see snow will be one you remember forever. The soft white carpet that's suddenly replaced the green of your back garden, the gentle fall of nature's purest white flakes. But all that's soon over as they grasp the possibilities. Sleds, snowballs, snow angels, and of course snowmen.

Just like sandcastles, there's a right and a wrong way to build a snowman. Crack it first time and you will receive their admiration forever – or at least until the thaw sets in.

1   You'll improve the odds if the snow is the right kind – not too fluffy, not too icy. Make a reasonable size snowball, then roll it along the ground to pick up more snow and add to its size. Keep going until you have a ball of between one and three feet in diameter. This will be your snowman's lower body

2   Repeat twice for the upper body and the head. Then, attach these to the top of the largest snowball so you have a large (lower body) medium (upper body) and small (head). Make sure these are attached properly, as there's nothing so ego-deflating as a decapitated snowman.

3   Make the nose with a carrot, eyes with pebbles or pieces of coal and a mouth with smaller pebbles. A hat and a scarf are obligatory clothing. Then stand back and enjoy the acclaim.

Build a sledge

With winter comes snow and a whole new type of adventure. If your children aren't busy building an igloo or skating, they'll be demanding to ride the powder like an Arctic explorer. In other words, they'll want a sledge.

You will need

- ❖ 0.6- x 1.2-m (2- x 4-ft), 2.5-cm- (1-in-) thick sheet of plywood (top board)
- ❖ A saw
- ❖ Sandpaper
- ❖ 2.5-cm- (1-in-) wide chisel or router with 2.5-cm- (1-in-) bit
- ❖ Two 0.3- x 1.2-m (1- x 4-ft), 2.5-cm- (1-in-) thick plywood (runners)
- ❖ Wood glue
- ❖ A screwdriver

- ❖ At least eight 5-cm (2-in) screws
- ❖ Four angle irons 15 cm (6 in) on each side, with at least four 0.5-cm ($\frac{1}{4}$-in) wide bolt holes
- ❖ A pencil
- ❖ Drill with 0.5-cm ($\frac{1}{4}$-in) bit
- ❖ At least 16 3-cm- (1$\frac{1}{2}$-in-) long, 0.5-cm ($\frac{1}{4}$-in) wide bolts with plenty of washers and nuts
- ❖ 0.5 m (2 ft) of rope

1 Take the top board and cut off the corners of one end with a saw. Round off the corners where you've cut with sandpaper to make a semicircle which will be the front of your sledge.

2 Use sandpaper to round off the back corners of the top board while you're there – rounded corners make falling off less painful.

3 Use a chisel or router to create two 2.5-cm- (1-in-) wide, 0.5-cm ($\frac{1}{4}$-in) deep grooves along the length of the top board, about 3 cm

(1½ in) in from the sides. The two plywood runners will fit into these grooves.

4   Stack the two runners on top of each other and cut off the top right and bottom left corners.

5   Sand the cut corners on both runners to make a smooth curve. This will run along the snow.

6   Place a thread of wood glue along the top edge of each runner and fit them into the grooves on the top board. Secure the runners in place by drilling screws down into them through the top board.

7   Turn the sledge upside down and lay the angle irons – iron strips bent at a right angle – in the corner between the runner and the bottom of the sledge. Use two angle irons for each runner, one at the front and one at the back. Use a pencil to mark the location of the bolt holes.

8   Remove the angle irons and drill holes all the way through the top board and runners where you have marked.

9   Secure the angle irons in place with bolts to hold the runners securely in place. Use washers on both sides of the board.

10 Drill a hole in the very front of your sledge, and loop the rope through it so you've got something to hold onto while you ride.

11 Decorate your sledge with paint and you're ready to go! For a sturdier structure, take your finished sledge to a blacksmith and have metal runners fitted over the wooden ones – that'll protect them from unexpected rocks lurking beneath the snow. You can also coat the whole structure in waterproof lacquer or polyurethane to keep water out of the wood and stop it rotting.

Choosing a pet

Pets are a part of growing up – but the sensible father is careful with his choice, and never agrees on a whim. The pet for you depends on many things, not least your surroundings and the amount of time you have to dedicate to its upkeep.

The age of your children is also important: more demanding pets should be left until your offspring is old enough to contribute to its care – start with pets that will look after themselves and work up. When your children are old enough let them help with feeding and mucking out.

Try your children out on other people's pets – you can always give them back! If you live in a flat, don't go for animals that love the great outdoors. And bear in mind who will be around in the day to look after them; if parents work and children are at school, then low-maintenance pets are obligatory. Cats may need a cat flap, and somewhere to put a litter tray – which can never be child-proof, so you must be aware of your youngest's whereabouts at all times.

Expense

Cost may be a factor. Aside from any price tag, dogs and cats require at least annual boosters and medical checks. They will also require neutering unless you want to deal with a whole houseful! Sickly animals can also be expensive – investigate pet insurance. And last but not least, there's food to consider.

If in doubt, go to the library and read up on your choices – or use the Internet. Then you will be ready to discuss the subject *en famille* with a reasonable amount of background knowledge at your disposal. Any pet is a responsibility, an addition to the family and an extra responsibility for Dad. So if in doubt, give it a little more time.

Go to a pet shop with the decision already made – do not be swayed by adorable looking pets that may be much more trouble than they appear. Even better, go to an animal sanctuary and re-home a cat or dog whose owner can no longer care for them. (Pedigree animals come with a premium price tag and are not for the beginner.)

Your choice

Choose wisely and you will see child and animal develop a bond that is part of growing up. Choose rashly and prepare for tears... Our suggestion is to start thinking long before you even mention the subject. And remember, as your child gets older and more things demand their time, you will become the pet owner – so it's important to choose something Dad likes too!

- ❖ **Low maintenance pets** – hamsters, guinea pigs, tortoises, goldfish, stick insects.
- ❖ **Medium maintenance pets** – cats, rabbits, rats, exotic fish, cage birds.
- ❖ **High maintenance pets** – dogs, horses, exotic animals/insects/ reptiles, and pedigree animals

Get a cat down from a tree

A dad's work is never done – certainly not if your family cat has just run up a tall tree and now can't quite work out how to get back down. Being able to rescue the cat from a tree will practically earn you the status of a hero in the eyes of your young children. Even if you don't own a cat, this is a useful thing to know so that you can help out your neighbours when it's their cat that has run up a tree. The general gratitude of the cat owner might not quite be worth the many cat scratches, but Dad shouldn't let that put him off.

You will need
- ❖ patience
- ❖ ladder
- ❖ leather work gloves
- ❖ pillowcase
- ❖ rope

1 The first thing to do is to stay calm (or try to get your neighbour to stay calm). If a cat is given privacy and time it will likely come down on its own. Give it a full night. In the meantime, keep the dog inside.

2 You can try calling to the cat at the base of the tree or opening a can of cat food to coax the beast down if you like but don't get frustrated if this has no effect. Cats are notorious for not listening or doing what they're asked.

3 If the cat is a kitten or it has a leash wrapped around its neck (for reasons that don't need to be disclosed) you'll have to

go get it. Kittens aren't strong enough to stay up in trees in high wind for very long.

4 First try to get the cat to come down on its own by leaning a wooden ladder up against the tree next to the cat. Leave it alone with the ladder for at least 15 minutes and see if the cat can work its own way down it.

5 If the cat is too freaked out to use the ladder, put on your work gloves to protect yourself from scratches (cats don't appreciate the fact that you're only trying to help) and take a pillowcase and a rope up the ladder with you.

6 When you reach the cat grab it by the nape of the neck to reduce your chances of getting scratched. This also has a calming effect on the creature.

7 You will find it extremely difficult to climb safely down a ladder while also holding a desperately struggling creature with claws, so gently put the cat in the pillowcase – an action which will undo the aforementioned calm – and secure it with the rope so that you can lower the cat down.

8 Next, lower the cat slowly to a person on the ground who is able to catch it.

9 Take the cat into the house before you let it out, lest it run up the tree again in a state of panic from getting put in a pillowcase.

Ride a horse

As a dad, you might never need to know how to ride a horse. Then again, you might prefer to know how to and never have to do it, than have to reluctantly admit your ignorance to your own children.

1 Make sure your stirrups are the right length. To measure, hold on to the stirrup buckle with one hand and pull out the length of the stirrup towards your armpit with the other hand. The stirrup iron should hit your armpit exactly.

2 Put one foot in the stirrup, grab hold of the horn and pommel of the saddle (the leather part sticking up right behind the horse's neck), and swing your other leg over the back of the horse. Be sure not to kick the horse during this motion or he's liable to kick you. Either that or take off with you hanging over the side.

3 Once you're sitting in the saddle, collect the reins and make sure both feet are in the stirrups.

4 Ask the horse to go by shouting out 'yee-ha' while waving your hat in the air. Just kidding. Simply squeeze your calves slightly and the beast will begin a slow paced walk.

5 If you would like to trot, squeeze the horse's side with your legs again. While the horse is trotting, you should post, which is rising about an inch in your saddle and then sitting again, to the rhythm of the horse's gait. A trot is a two beat gait. Failure to post equals a rough ride and a very sore rear end.

6 To stop, squeeze the reins and sit deep; you may have to lean back a bit and put your weight into your behind and heels. Don't ever pull on the bit. Horses don't like that.

Never sit or kneel near a horse, and always approach a horse from the front or side, never from the rear. Never stand directly behind a horse. If you are walking behind one, make sure to keep your distance so that you are out of range in case it suddenly kicks out.

Learning to swim

Teaching your child to swim gives you quality time together and imparts a skill that will stay with him forever and could save a life. What's equally important, in the short term at least, is that it's a fun experience for Dad and offspring alike. The only downside is having to appear in swimming costume in public, so start doing those sit-ups . . .

Top swimming tips

- ❖ Start early before the memory of the liquid-filled womb fades and fears set in.
- ❖ Have a regular time every week you visit the pool. Most will have parent and child sessions clearly allotted.
- ❖ Start in the teaching pool, playing games in the shallow water before graduating to deeper water.
- ❖ Do not force your child to put his head in the water. Start by blowing bubbles and he will follow your example.
- ❖ Have your child push off from the bottom and end up in your arms, staying within easy reach.
- ❖ Make friends. Bringing other parents and children or making friends with those already there will relax your child.
- ❖ Make sure you are one on one with your child. If there's more than one involved, get your better half to come in too.
- ❖ While encouraging your kids enjoy the water, make sure they are also aware of the dangers. Never take them deeper than they are comfortable; comfort and confidence are your goals.

Learning to dive

You're not a dad if you haven't embarrassed the kids with a water-splashing belly flop or two on holiday. But sooner or later they're going to want to know how to dive properly. So listen up!

1 Start on the side of the pool from a sitting position. Your child can work your way up to a standing dive and, finally, the diving board.

2 Sit her on the edge of the pool with feet in the water. Lower her head so that her chin touches her chest. Clasp her hands together, place them on the water surface, aimed toward the bottom and from this position, roll her into the water.

3 Next, have her kneel on both knees on the edge of the pool. Keeping her head down and aiming her hands at the bottom of the pool, she leans forward and fall into the water, head down at all times.

4 The final poolside dive is achieved by standing on one leg on the edge of the pool, holding the other to the rear. She may need you to lift her rear leg and aim her toward the water. Their priority should be to go up in the air rather than as far out as she can. When mastered without anyone's help, she is on her way to springboard diving.

Main rules to remember

- ❖ Straighten legs, making sure knees are not bent.
- ❖ Her head should be down between her arms.
- ❖ Hands should be together and fingers pointed.
- ❖ Tell her to bend at the waist until she falls in like a rolling football.
- ❖ Make sure to keep her chin tucked in, or she will hit the water in a painful belly flop.

Advanced Dad

- ❖ Fixing a watch
- ❖ Changing a tyre
- ❖ Letting children win at games
- ❖ Telling bad jokes
- ❖ Finding time for yourself

Once the initial fears of fatherhood have been banished forever, it's time to flex your wings and take on some more ambitious tasks, from advanced DIY projects to bonding over sports, and from honing your ability to embarass your child to finding a bit of time for yourself. There's no syllabus or certificate for the Advanced Dad, but the glow of pride is often more than sufficient. Give yourself a pat on the back – you've earned it.

Fix a DVD player

Any problem with your television equipment is enough to ratchet family tensions to breaking point – the only movie night you and Mum have been able to arrange for a month; a crucial soap opera is about to air; or the little ones have just been promised their favourite cartoons and a tantrum is going to erupt any moment. The pressure is bound to be more than any self-respecting dad can stand. As ever, the challenge is to keep your cool and save the day.

The good news is, most problems with TVs, videos and DVDs are down to loose or wrongly made connections. So your first step is to check everything is snugly plugged in to where it should be, check that none of the fuses in the plugs have blown, and using a table lamp, check sockets and extension leads are working.

Batteries required

If you're pounding your remote control and having no luck, the obvious first step is to replace the batteries. If that doesn't help, try getting to within 50 centimetres of the remote control sensor on the

DVD player. If all else fails, try turning the lights off – it's been reported that some long life energy-saver bulbs can interfere with remote controls.

It sounds simple, but if you're getting no video or DVD playback, check that your TV is set to the correct channel and your AV receiver is set to the correct input channel. No sound? Check your volume control! Human error is often at fault.

If a DVD won't play, then press eject, re-seat and re-insert the disc. In about 80 per cent of cases the problem will disappear with this very simple manoeuvre.

Regional rules

There may be a regional incompatibility between the disc and your player. Check the small print – Region 0 discs are not restricted, others may be.

Some DVD players have a fault which turns subtitles on inappropriately. It is worth going into your player's set-up menu and changing the subtitle language from Auto to English. This should stop at least some of these occurrences.

Sticky situation

If it sticks, check the surface and wipe clean with a soft cloth or tissue, working from the centre out. Still nothing? Try a disc that you know worked recently. If that works, the problem lies with the new one, rather than the machine. If it doesn't it's worth checking a second, and even a third. If none of them work, it's likely that the problem is with the machine and you'll need to take it to an expert.

Fix a stopped watch

Watches that don't work are no good to anybody, but there are a couple of things you can try to get it going again. The battery may have corroded, preventing good electrical contact with the terminals in the watch. You can try an ink (not pencil) eraser, on the contact surfaces – it contains very fine grit which makes it act like sandpaper, removing the surface corrosion to get to the base metal of the contacts. Do the same with the surfaces of the battery. If that fails, maybe a new battery is the only answer.

There are two kinds of watch, electro-mechanical and digital. The latter is more or less impossible for even the most expert dad to fix, while the former may have dust in the mechanism, preventing the motor from turning, or its lubrication may have dried out and gummed up the works. In this case, go to a jeweller and have the mechanism cleaned.

Hints for a longer-lasting watch

- ❖ Avoid shocks (such as dropping it on hard surfaces). Normal shocks caused by sports like tennis will not harm the watch.
- ❖ Protect it from perspiration by wiping it dry as soon as possible.
- ❖ Avoid extreme temperatures. Mechanical watches are more affected by extremes of temperature than quartz watches.
- ❖ Avoid exposure to chemical substances that may change the colour of cases, bracelets and straps.

If all else fails, Dad can still have the final word. Because even a stopped watch is right twice a day.

Unblock a toilet

There's little more distressing at any age than a blocked loo – even if some of us are fortunate enough to have more than one bathroom these days. Serious measures are called for.

1 Stop flushing. It will only add more water to the problem and may cause the bowl to overflow and flood the bathroom.
2 Cut off the water supply. Find an indoor stopcock on the cold water pipe near the toilet. Alternatively, lifting the ball valve in the cistern will ensure water cannot enter.
3 Cover the floor with newspapers or old towels.
4 Put on rubber gloves.
5 If toilet bowl is full, remove some of the water to a bucket.
6 Locate the obstruction. If it can be seen, wrap a bin-liner around your arm and hand and try to pull it out.
7 Try to move the obstruction. If you can't see the blockage then try using a plunger to create suction which draws out the blockage and assists its passage down the drain. Alternatively a straightened-out coat hanger with the hook end pointing away from you may help loosen the blockage and help it go down the pipes. An augur or toilet snake is a more professional version of this.
8 Check the toilet is clear. Pour some water from the bucket into the bowl to see if it is safe to flush.
9 Disinfect the toilet.
10 If the toilet remains blocked, reluctantly admit defeat and call in a plumber.

Put up a shelf

It is important to get this one right, as shelf failure inevitably involves tears and breakages. Make sure yours stay up, or Dad's reputation will, like the sorry piece of wood, reside firmly at floor level.

1   The first problem to address is how the supporting brackets will be secured to the wall. This will depend on the type of wall. A brick wall will need a masonry drill and wall plugs, while a hollow indoor wall should be drilled where they are attached to the studs (vertical timbers). These are usually 16 inches to two feet apart.

2   Where a short shelf is being fitted, it is easier to fit the brackets to the shelf before drilling the holes in the wall. If more than one shelf is to be fitted, ensure the relative position of the brackets is the same on each shelf.

3   Lay the shelf upside-down on a flat surface, like a table, and against a vertical surface like a wall. This will ensure that the back of the bracket verticals are in line with the back of the shelf.

4   Fix the brackets to the shelf making sure the screws you use are not so long that they'll break through the shelf itself.

5   Put the shelf in position against the wall at the required height. If more than one shelf is being fitted, start with the uppermost one. Use a spirit level to make sure the shelf is horizontal.

6   Use the fixing holes in the vertical bracket to mark the positions for the holes to be drilled in the wall. Place in position and use the spirit level as a check.

7   Remove the shelf, drill the wall as necessary, and fix the shelf in position using the appropriate wall plugs and screws.

Build a shed

There's nothing quite like having a place of your own where you can get away from it all, and a garden shed is a great place for dad-related activities that Mum might not want done in the house. Firstly check that you don't need planning permission. Then get hold of a building plan, either from a book, magazine or the Internet, that does not exceed your DIY capabilities, or buy a ready made kit. Then all you have to do is follow the instructions to create your own castle. Sort of. Here are some tips to make the most of your shed.

- ❖ Your foundation can be a wooden skid on a gravel base that drains well and helps keep the timber dry, or a concrete slab. To prepare the gravel base, remove four inches of soil in an area 12 inches wider and longer than the shed dimension. Fill with gravel, rake and pat down until it is fairly level, then check using a spirit level and straight length of wood.
- ❖ Most of the framing can be done with a mitre saw. The nails used for the framing are called common nails. These have a larger diameter than box nails, making them stronger and more effective.
- ❖ Roofing means installing roof sheathing, fascia boards and shingles. Asphalt shingles are the most durable and low maintenance material available to roof your shed.
- ❖ Plywood siding is the least expensive and easiest to install. Try to obtain vertical board siding which has a lip edge as this forms weatherproof vertical seams.
- ❖ To protect your shed from the elements apply protective finish, stain, paint, or varnish as soon as possible.

Change a tyre

Getting a flat tyre in the middle of nowhere is bad. Not knowing how to change it is worse. This is one of the basics every would-be hero should know. And remember, it's not uncommon for grown men to stand on wrenches to loosen and tighten wheel nuts, so don't hesitate to do this if necessary.

You will need
- ❖ flathead screwdriver
- ❖ wheel wrench
- ❖ jack
- ❖ spare tyre

1 Remove spare tyre, wheel wrench, jack and screwdriver from the trunk.
2 If you have a hubcap, use the screwdriver or the flat end of your wheel wrench to pry it off.
3 Use the wheel wrench to loosen the nuts on the flat tyre. Do not remove them yet. Once you've loosened the first nut, do the nut directly opposite, and continue with the others in this way.
4 Place the jack near the tyre you're changing. (Most owner's manuals show the proper placement.)
5 Jack up the car until there's enough room to remove the flat tyre and replace the spare.
6 Remove the nuts from the flat tyre and pull the tyre off.
7 Replace with spare. Lower the car, replace and tighten the wheel nuts.

Always make sure you have a properly inflated spare tyre and a working jack in your car before you set off, so that you're not stuck if you do get a flat. When you stop to change the tyre, find a safe place to pull over, and put your hazard lights on so that you're not putting yourself or other road users in danger.

Teach your child to drive

As the bumper sticker says, We were all learners once: thanks for
your patience. So dads must stay cool, calm, collected – and firmly in
the passenger seat – as they attempt to pass on this very important
life skill. Driving is a rite of passage of growing up, so don't resort to
insults or name-calling when problems occur, as they inevitably will.
Be patient and wait for things to calm down.

Getting started

Before you put your life in their hands, you should arrange for your
teenager to have a few proper lessons with a driving instructor to get
her started. It is better for her to learn the practical parts of driving
from a professional who has the patience to explain the idea behind
parallel parking.

You may decide to dodge the mental stresses and strains of
white-knuckle rides with your teenager and just entrust her to a
driving instructor from the outset, but you'll find that it's helpful for
her to have the extra practice with you.

Off-road training

Hand, eye and foot co-ordination are all essential if your child is going
to pass her test and stay safe on the road. The best place to learn
these is off the road well away from traffic – a disused airfield, empty
car park (try a trading estate at weekends) or other tarmacked
surface. It's best to keep your seatbelt on at all times, as should your
new learner.

Help them cope

Starting the engine and getting a feel for the car is a major trial for the first-time driver, and odds are you're old enough to have forgotten how hard this can actually be.

Encourage the new driver when she does something right and keep an even tone to your voice as you correct her errors. Don't let your irritation, annoyance or even fear show. Once she has located all the gears and can brake on command, it's time to try the open road. Try at all times to encourage her to look to the horizon, beyond the end of the bonnet which is her default focus. Night driving can be attempted once daytime confidence is established.

As well as supplying your learner with the Highway Code, a good purchase is a computer software CD that encourages her to look out for hazards and increase her awareness. It's never too soon for her to imagine herself behind the wheel and develop the road sense you take for granted.

Under the bonnet

Almost as important as driving skills in the general scheme of things is understanding the way the car works. Take her to the garage and have her put the petrol in, guiding her firmly away from the colour-coded diesel pump (unless you're a diesel-engined car, of course). Then open the bonnet and show her the different holes in which the oil and windscreen washer liquid are inserted. Tyre pressure and treadwear checks are another good habit to get into – this is not only a safety consideration as properly inflated tyres increase fuel economy.

Barbecues

Children love food, and the outdoors – so barbecues were made for them. But it's down to Dad to keep control, so there are some handy hints to keep in mind as you light the flames.

Safety first

First and foremost, make sure your children are aware of the dangers of hot coals, potentially very hot food and never let the little ones have a go at cooking. That's Dad's job! Get them setting out paper plates, serviettes and cutlery while everything cooks

Make sure the barbecue is on a firm, level surface before lighting. Once it's lit, don't move it. The grill should be in a position where it will be sheltered from the wind – but not where the smoke and fumes will be blown into the house! Avoid overhanging branches and foliage, too. Never pour flammable fluid on a barbecue to hasten the flames. Sit back and be patient.

Rules of meat

1 Make sure meat is fully defrosted before placing it on the grill.
2 Pre-cook chicken in the microwave or oven beforehand, using the barbecue to finish it off.
3 Don't let chicken wings and drumsticks cool down before putting them on the barbecue though; poultry should never be reheated once it has cooled.
4 When you take meat off the barbecue, such as burgers, sausages and poultry, make sure it is cooked all the way

Barbecues are a family affair, so remember to include some child-friendly foods, such as corn on the cob cut into kid-size segments, vegetable kebabs, garlic bread or pitta with salsa topping, spare ribs, homemade burgers, chicken drumsticks and bananas grilled in their peels, served with ice cream.

through, with no trace of pink in the juices or inside when you open
one up to test.

5 Of course always remember to wash your hands after handling raw
meat before touching other food, and don't use the same utensils
for raw ingredients and cooked food.

6 To avoid cross-contamination, always keep raw foods to be cooked
away from the foods ready to eat.

Cooking hints and tips

❖ If marinating, pat the meat dry with paper towels so it cooks
evenly.

❖ If using a water smoker or an aluminium pan in the grill, always
use hot water. That way the water is already able to steam and
you are not wasting fuel by heating cold water.

❖ Always use a thermometer to regulate the grill temperature.

❖ If the cooking temperature needs to be increased you must add
lighted charcoal to the existing fire; do not add un-lit charcoal.

❖ Try not to lift the cover and peek unless you are adding lighted
charcoal or basting as the more you
lift, the longer the food will take
to cook. Add wood chunks
(if you are using them) or
charcoal at the same time
you baste the meat.

Teach your child chess

There's no better game to encourage concentration and logical thought than chess. The first task is to work out where the pieces start on the board. That's enough of a first lesson for most people. Let her mirror your movements as you set up the pieces, then change roles. Once she knows how the board is set up, then concentrate on how each major piece works. Add this to what you already know, one piece at a time.

- ❖ Use draughts/checkers, a simpler game, as a stepping stone. The rules are different but it's not that confusing.
- ❖ If you can see her make a mistake, help her guess what it is and correct it.
- ❖ Explain what's happened when you win, then go back over the last few moves and show her alternatives.
- ❖ Turn the board around after a time and let your student play with the majority of the pieces. This 'turning the tables' tactic puts you at a potentially fatal disadvantage.
- ❖ Use two clocks to give her a time advantage over you. You may make errors or run out of time, while she can use her extra thinking space to outwit you.
- ❖ Set up an easy ending – her with two rooks and a king, you with king only – and give her a time or move limit to checkmate you.
- ❖ Practise a little every day – then when your child is old enough buy her a computer program to play against.

Letting your child win at games

There's nothing worse than a bad loser – and it's important your child can learn to take defeat with a smile. But are there times when you should let your child win?

When you're teaching her a new and challenging game, for example, chess, she will be encouraged by a win here and there rather than setting up knowing she is going to lose, so to keep her interested in playing you might want to consider occasionally throwing the game, just until she's got the hang of it. No-one enjoys losing, and the maxim 'it's not whether you win or lose it's how you play the game' is a mighty big sentence for a little person to swallow. She also needs to learn how to win gracefully and not rub her opponents' nose in it. Rubbing Dad's nose, of course, is all part of the fun.

Even the odds

Playing games where chance plays a greater part than skill can even things up of course – snakes and ladders and many card games are examples. And needless to say it's crucial if you are 'fixing' the result that the child isn't old enough to realise this. Otherwise their genuine wins will be devalued.

As you get older, games of skill could involve a handicap, as in golf where you 'give' your less experienced opponent shots. Handicaps can inject a genuine excitement into the game, and of course can be reduced as your protégé gains in skill and confidence. After all, you wouldn't want her to win every time, would you?

Touchline etiquette

Supportive parents have played an important part in the lives of most sporting heroes. But when you take your son and daughter to play their sport of choice at the weekend, bear the following in mind to avoid becoming a sporting dad from hell!

- ❖ Stay at least two metres from the touchline. It is important that players have enough space to take their throws, while linesmen need a good view of the line to judge whether the ball is in or out of play.
- ❖ Don't stand anywhere that will distract her.
- ❖ Don't yell instructions. It is confusing for players when there's a barrage of instructions from a variety of voices. Let the coaches do their job.
- ❖ Applaud good play or attempts to be creative by both team.
- ❖ Let your child take part in the pre- and post-match rituals by arriving early and leaving only when she is dismissed by the coach.
- ❖ Give your child the same praise and love when she loses as when she wins. She'll need it! Keep your comments constructive and maybe leave them until later in the day if she is really disappointed.
- ❖ Make friends with other parents. You might end up with a social life of your own.

Watching sports with a child

The expression 'it's only a game' has been used by wives through the ages who just don't understand the importance of sport. Dads, of course, know better. But whether you're watching a live event or just the television, how you react will do a lot to shape your child's reaction to those twin impostors of triumph and disaster.

1 Keep the language clean at all times.
2 Don't run down the referee, umpire or judge's eyesight or judgement. A regard for authority is important.
3 Always give credit for good play, even by the opposition. Even if you choke on the words.
4 Give your child a few pointers she wouldn't normally enjoy. She'll thank you for it one day.
5 If your child shows an interest, suggest you go out and have a backyard game of whatever sport it is you are watching.
6 Don't drink alcohol or smoke – it associates these habits with the sport, and the glamour will rub off.
7 Ask your child for her opinion instead of giving her the benefit of yours all the time.
8 If it's a sport she's tried at school, explain how watching professionals can improve her own game.
9 Young children have a limited attention span. About six or seven is the best age to start watching together.
10 If you simply can't control your innermost frustration, switch off and take a walk round the block. You can't admit it to the wife, but it *is* only a game…

When watching or playing sport with your child, teach her about the importance of sportsmanship, both as a player and a participant. She needs to know it's wrong to cheat, lose your temper and be a bad loser (or a bad winner). And then remember to lead by example. She has to learn to take bad luck and disappointment in her stride.

Supporting the right team

The right team for your child, of course, will be the one you support. Dads have a nose for these things. But there's nothing wrong with a bit of encouragement to make your kids' choice that much easier and domestic harmony that much more certain.

It's important to get her along to a proper match; armchair sports fans can have the pick of the litter, but there's nothing like a day out. And when you've been to the 'real thing', it narrows your choices down somewhat. These tactics will work 90 per cent of the time. The rest of the time your child will pick the team that's furthest away just to spite you. In which case, you'll just have to grin and bear it, especially when her team beats yours!

❖ Join a supporters club or other organisation with a membership card or badge. This will increase the feeling of belonging.

❖ If your team is a local one, get involved. There's always something to be done, from painting the stadium in the close season to helping out on matchdays by selling programmes, shaking a fundraising bucket or helping in the shop.

❖ Get there nice and early and enjoy the build-up to the game. Often that's the best bit!

❖ Work your way up to the expensive shirt. When it gets to that point let her choose her own name to be printed on, but buy at the beginning of the season (clubs often change designs later in the season) and only when there's no chance their current hero could be heading for pastures new. Or even your local rivals!

Wolf-whistling

If you foresee a future career change to building construction, or you're planning to hail a few cabs in New York City, you'll need to learn this one. Anyway, it's good fun to show off to anyone who can't do it, and often an advantage to know how to whistle loud – which is what you get when you use your fingers and your mouth for the wolf whistle. You never know when you'll need to make noise for the home side.

Not everyone can master the wolf whistle, at least not straight away, but keep trying and you'll get there.

1 Tuck your lips inwards so they cover your teeth and are tucked back into your mouth.
2 Place two fingers of your choice between the corners and centre of your mouth (you can use the thumb and middle finger of either hand, your right and left index fingers, or your right and left pinkie fingers). They should be one knuckle into your mouth.
3 Angle your fingernails inwards towards the centre of your tongue and make your lips firm.
4 Angle the tongue by drawing it back so that the front touches the bottom of your mouth a short distance from your gums.
5 Blow.

Give your child a nickname

Dads beware! If you want to see a face of utter horror, try using your child's family nickname in front of her classmates. The mortified look she adopt is one that will stay in your memory forever. But nicknames happen, and should probably be kept within the family. Here are some tips.

- ❖ Names given to your child pre-birth are rarely welcomed once they are no longer a lump!
- ❖ An aspirational nickname connected with a hobby is always acceptable – eg a famous footballer or a guitar player.
- ❖ Anything with 'little' in it guarantees she'll end up bigger than you!
- ❖ Don't try to be hip and use street slang… there's nothing more embarrassing!

Telling bad jokes

Fathers are expected to be the source of bad humour. But expect some abuse as you carry out this time-honoured duty!

- ❖ It's all about timing. Make sure that's good even if the joke is not.
- ❖ Don't ask permission nor tell everyone how funny the joke is beforehand; just go ahead.
- ❖ If you don't get a laugh, plough on regardless.
- ❖ Use joke websites to replenish your store of bad humour.
- ❖ Don't tell a joke you don't understand.

Karaoke

Singing with your children is a great experience – and even if you don't have the next teen winner in the family it's amazing what fun they and you can get out of a song. There are a range of DVD discs available that project lyrics onto your screen while playing backing tracks to be sung over. You can also get karaoke-based computer games.

Spotting young talent

It's never too early to start, either, as there are now even toddlers' favourites such as 'Baa Baa Black Sheep' and 'Rock-a-Bye Baby' available that are suitable from eight months to three years old. So you can encourage your child's singing talent, not to mention love of karaoke, from an early age. Sing-a-longs can also help young children with their reading skills.

Going public

The next step will be finding a proper karaoke night to take them to (or drag them to) where you can all merrily showcase your family talent. The key thing to remember when you're singing is, don't get embarrassed – it's just a bit of fun, and your children are probably embarrassed enough for the both of you.

Dancing like a dad

Let's face it, you'll never make one of those celebrity TV dance shows. So why not do what comes naturally and embarrass your offspring by dancing like a dad? There are some crucial moves to master, so wise up and don't disappoint your public.

The Grass Cutter	Swing an imaginary hover mower from side to side, nimbly removing your feet from the line of flight.
The Barman	No natural rhythm – no problem! Pull a few imaginary pints – you may need them after all this exertion.
The Plumber	The roof's leaking there . . . and there . . . and there. Reach for the imaginary holes and John Travolta's your uncle. Also known as squirty dancing.
The Left-Footed Waltz	Ever tried to waltz with another man? It's a recipe for disaster but one the assembled multitude will lap up. The question is, are you man enough to take the jibes?
The Macarena	The one they made especially for dads! Study the hand movements if you dare, but don't expect to get them right.
Agadoo	It doesn't matter if they play the song or not – 'Push pineapple, shake the tree' is a motto to live, and dance, by. Get shakin'.
The Twist	Big in your own Dad's time, but a risky business unless your back is in A1 shape. A visit to the chiropractor is a very real possibility if things go horribly wrong.

Dad's musical tastes

Remember your dad's reaction to your music. Negative, no doubt. And of course that was in the days when music was music. So the question is how to ensure harmony in the home – the answer, getting your children to like what Dad likes.

Bear in mind that the music you play when your kids are growing up will have a big effect on their tastes. They'll either follow in your musical footsteps or rebel against you totally!

- ❖ Note which songs in the charts are cover versions and dig out the originals. Your kids can also enjoy extra kudos by pointing out the fact to their friends.
- ❖ Keep only your music in the car. Then they have to listen to your choice if only on the way to and from school.
- ❖ Identify their natural musical leanings towards dance music, melodic music or harmonies and play them something from your collection they will relate to.
- ❖ When trying to engage their interest, start with the real classics from your day, which always tend to go down well, like the Beatles, James Taylor, Jack Johnson and Bob Marley.
- ❖ Don't pour scorn on their taste in music. At the end of the day everyone has the right to listen to what they want to. The music industry has probably moved on without you and you'll just have to accept that your musical tastes aren't in anymore.

Judging the right tone to take with your child may be the hardest part. Remember that teenagers think they are grown up, even if you still see them as your little ones, so try to treat them like an equal during discussions such as these. Nothing kills a conversation like a parent who talks down to his child.

The birds and the bees talk

Your child is exposed to sex and sexuality every time they watch TV. Sometimes it seems that every commercial from toothpaste to jeans is about attracting the opposite sex. So it's never too early to start talking – even if the thought brings you out in a cold sweat.

Don't judge

Children need to know that you aren't going to judge them, that you love and accept them no matter what they tell you. Remember your own childhood and the mistakes you made. All you can do is help them avoid some of yours – there will be others to take their place.

Starting the conversation is the hardest part. Ask how they feel about what is going on in their lives or the world in general. Tell them the dangers of jumping into a sexual relationship before they are ready. Talk to them about how to handle themselves when they get into situations where they are being pressured to have sex.

Discussion points

It's important to give them a healthy perspective of sexuality. Let your teens know that how they dress or act will give people an impression of them that may be different to what they assume.

Discuss standards and make a list of standards you all agree on. If nothing else it will remind you of some of the points you may have conflicts about that still need to be resolved.

There is no guarantee that your teenagers won't make mistakes, but keeping the lines of communication open may mean that they will come to you when they need answers or help.

Meet prospective partners

It's sometimes hard to accept our little darlings are now finding darlings of their own – especially when it comes to daughters. The prospects for embarrassment are huge, so if in doubt say nothing. If that's impossible here are a few handy hints to bear in mind as the introductions are made. And don't forget – you were once on the receiving end!

Dos and don'ts

- ❖ Do make sure your first meeting is on neutral territory. That way everyone's on the same level, and there's less formality.
- ❖ Do find out their interests to make sure conversation flows.
- ❖ Do encourage them to speak freely; nod and smile a lot, you'll look less fierce.
- ❖ Do how an interest in their family.
- ❖ Do avoid discussing their relationship with your offspring.
- ❖ Don't get out the baby pictures.
- ❖ Don't talk about religion or politics.
- ❖ Don't dress too formally or too casually.
- ❖ Don't judge by appearances. Get to know the person behind the appearance and ignore the ear/nose rings.
- ❖ Don't tell tales of your own courtship; that's just too much information.
- ❖ Never under any circumstances mention or compare them to your child's former boy/girlfriends.

Time for yourself

Taking time for yourself can be for various reasons. You might want to catch up with friends at a pub, or go watch a movie or simply relax and take a drive. It may also be that if you don't pay attention to yourself, your health will start to fail. High stress, little or no sleep and no exercise will weaken your immune system and invite sickness, not to mention zap creative energy and slow you down at work. And if you feel bad, chances are you're not looking your best either. Bags under the eyes, two-day stubble and wrinkled clothes are just a few signs that you need to put down the baby and step away from the changing table.

Ten signs you need help

1   You fall asleep under the baby gym while your little one is playing.
2   You show up at work with vomit stains on your shirt and don't care.
3   Everyone you see asks if there's been a death in the family.
4   Dinner has become your infant's leftover rice cereal.
5   You fall asleep in the drive-through at the fast food restaurant.
6   You freshen yourself up with a nappy wipe.
7   Cold coffee becomes 'not that bad'.
8   Plants wilt when you breathe on them.
9   You forget your baby's name when the shop assistant asks about it.
10 You drive to the doctor's office for the three-month check-up and forget to put the baby in the car.

Romance Mum

With a new baby waking up at all hours of the night and the stresses of work in full swing, lots of things start to fall by the wayside, including house cleaning, gardening, reading the paper and of course, romance. What's worse is that while the dirty dishes and clothes will visibly stack up, there aren't many overt warning signs that your relationship is going sour. Plus, it'll be no surprise that both of you would rather sleep when the baby is asleep instead of staying up to watch a movie or talk. The danger is that these things continue to happen. That's why it's important to carve out some time for you and the missus.

- ❖ Take the initiative by bringing home flowers occasionally.
- ❖ After you put your baby down at night, sit with your partner, even if it's just for five minutes, and talk about your day.
- ❖ Get your parents (or hers) to come and practise their grand-parenting skills while you take the night off together.
- ❖ Rub her shoulders, even if it's just for five minutes.
- ❖ Make dinner together and sit down to eat it together. Candles and a bottle of wine would also help.
- ❖ Take her on a surprise romantic picnic – even if it's just in the backyard.
- ❖ Try to arrange a babysitter and instigate a date night once a week. If you're having trouble fitting it into your schedule then change your schedule. After all, this is the relationship you started with, and when the kids leave home to explore their own lives it'll be the relationship you have in the end. That's the idea anyway.

Things your dad taught you

Before you open your mouth to impart knowledge to your offspring, consider these gems that your dad probably told you. You may decide silence is the better option!

Individuality	'I'll bet if all your friends jumped off a bridge, you would too.'
Religion	'You'd better pray that stain will come out of that carpet!'
Behaviour	'Stop acting like an idiot!'
Logic	'Because I said so – that's why.'
Envy	'There are millions of less fortunate children in this world who don't have wonderful parents like you do.'
Stamina	'You'll sit there until all that food is finished!'
Problem solving	'If I yelled because I saw a meteor coming towards you, would you listen to me then?'
Weather	'It looks like a tornado swept through your room!'
Hypocrisy	'If I've told you once, I've told you a million times, don't exaggerate!'
Osmosis	'Shut your mouth and eat your supper.'

Dad's Chair: make your own space

Used to be you were the centre of attention – now you have to carve out a dad-shaped niche for yourself in a house that's run for the benefit of your offspring. Stake out your space, keeping cats, dogs and kids off the chair in question and surround with the following.

Staking your territory

First stake out your personal territory – mark it out with the appropriate furniture. A **footstool on** which to place your slippered feet is of course essential, as is a side table, for various accumulated dad clutter. And obviously the most comfortable chair in the house. Preferably one that reclines if possible.

Accessories for dad

Dad's space will need certain accessories to truly put his stamp on it, and make sure everything he needs is close to hand. A favourite cushion helps to mark the chair as yours. Even better if you have one left over from Father's Day that actually says 'Dad' on it. Bring in a newspaper and magazine rack so that you can stay abreast of world events. Make sure the designated spot for the television remotes is within easy reach (you may need to reeducate your family on where exactly this spot should be). Add in a stash of edible treats, like peanuts, (you never know where the next meal is going to come from!), and you're good to go.

Pipe and slippers: the complete dad outfit

Beware Father's Day and birthdays – your wife and kids will be trying to give you a style makeover. Avoid this at all costs. Stick with the tried and trusted and you can't go wrong.

Essentials of a dad's wardrobe

Slippers	Clichéd they may be, but after a long day at work swapping shoes for slippers says you're home.
Shirt	The older the better, really – style like yours never goes out of fashion. And if it does, it'll be back in eventually.
Tie	These are very handy in an emergency – like when your belt buckle breaks or the dog loses the lead.
Trousers	Comfort is the watchword here. The width of the leg is not as important as room at the top. Elasticated waists rule.
Socks	The perennial Christmas present for the imaginatively challenged. Strange how you've got so many odd pairs, but that's life.
Pipe	Health and safety don't like it, but if a man can't enjoy himself in his own home… Just make sure not to do it under those pesky smoke detectors.

Index